The Rainmaker Effect

Stefan Kühl is professor of sociology at the University of Bielefeld in Germany and works as a consultant for Metaplan, a consulting firm based in Princeton, Hamburg, Shanghai, Singapore, Versailles and Zurich. He studied sociology and history at the University of Bielefeld (Germany), Johns Hopkins University in Baltimore (USA), Université Paris-X-Nanterre (France) and the University of Oxford (UK).

Other Books by Stefan Kühl

Organizations: A Systems Approach
(Routledge 2013)
Ordinary Organizations: Why Normal Men Carried Out the Holocaust
(Polity Press 2016)
When the Monkeys Run the Zoo: The Pitfalls of Flat Hierarchies
(Organizational Dialogue Press 2017)
Work: Marxist and Systems-Theoretical Approaches
(Routledge 2019)
Sisyphus in Management: The Futile Search for the Optimal Organizational Structure
(Organizational Dialogue Press 2020)

To contact us:

Metaplan
101 Wall Street
Princeton, NJ 08540
USA
Phone: +1 609-688-9171
stefankuehl@metaplan.com
www.metaplan.com

Stefan Kühl

The Rainmaker Effect
Contradictions of the Learning Organization

Organizational Dialogue Press
Princeton, Hamburg, Shanghai, Singapore, Versailles, Zurich

ISBN (Print) 978-1-7323861-6-7
ISBN (EPUB) 978-1-7323861-7-4

Copyright © 2019 by Stefan Kühl

All rights reserved. No part of this publication may be reproduced or transmitted in any form or by any means, without permission in writing from the author.

Translated by: Adam Blauhut
Cover Design: Guido Klütsch
Typesetting: Thomas Auer
Project Management: Tabea Koepp
www.organizationaldialoguepress.com

Contents

Preface:
On Rainmakers, Change Projects,
and Management Concepts...9

1.
Introduction: The Limits of the Learning Organization.... 15

2.
The End of the Dream of the
Optimal Organizational Structure...23

    2.1. An Initial Approach to Solving the Dilemma of Stability and Change: Stable Organizational Structures with Change-Oriented Units..25
    2.2. The Problem with the Optimal Organizational Structure—Sealed-Off Cores..37
    2.3. The End of the Hope for an Optimal Organizational Structure—Confronting a Turbulent Environment................44

3.
The Learning Organization and the Hope
For "Good" Rules of Change...52

    3.1. The Learning Organization—New Methods for Resolving the Dilemma of Stability and Change..........................54
    3.2. Signs of the Rationality of Change..62
    3.3. From Rational Organizational Architectures to the Principles of Rational Change..69

4.
The Blind Spots of the Learning Organization—Seven Contradictions in the Rules of Good Organizational Change 74

4.1. The Dilemma of Objectives—Precisely Defined Goals Provide Guidance, but Reduce Adaptability 85
4.2. The Identification Dilemma—Identifying with Change Processes Reduces Organizational Elasticity 91
4.3. The Employee Dilemma—When the Focus Is on People 99
4.4. The Dilemma of Communication—the Strengths and Weaknesses of Discussion 107
4.5. The Dilemma of Self-Organization—When Self-Organization Is Determined by Organization by Others 115
4.6. The Dilemma of Reserves—the Demand for Self-Obstruction 118
4.7. The Learning Dilemma—When Organizations Fall Victim to Successful Learning 124
4.8 The Limitations of Planned Organizational Change 132

5.
On the Benefits and Dangers of the Irrationality, Ignorance, and Forgetfulness of the Learning Organization 137

5.1. The Art of Treating Uncertain Knowledge as Certain 144
5.2. The Learning Organization Concept—Organized Self-Pacification 151
5.3. The Learning Trap—the Learning Organization and Crises 161

6.
Beyond the Learning Organization—
Managing the Dilemma of Organizational Change 165

6.1. The Argument for an Overarching Perspective—
Managing Contradictions 166

6.2. Beyond the Dream of a Change Process That Can Be Planned 175

An Afterword on Methodology 178

Bibliography 179

Preface:
On Rainmakers, Change Projects, and Management Concepts

This book project began with a puzzling observation I made when analyzing a number of projects in the Central African Republic. These focused on economic promotion, infrastructure development, and health education. During my analysis I noticed a discrepancy between the official accounts and the everyday reality of the project participants. Whereas the project proposals, plans, and descriptions focused on principles such as self-organization, participation, ongoing communication, continuous learning, and clear objectives, the projects themselves appeared to function according to their own set of rules, which were contradictory and contested. The positive-sounding models around which these projects were ostensibly organized had little in common with the reality perceived by the participants.

It seemed obvious to attribute this dual reality to the difficult political and economic context of development projects in general, and to the consequences of civil war, postcolonial administrative structures, corrupt officials, and partially incompetent project teams in Central Africa, in particular. However, I later realized that my experience with Central African development projects did not differ fundamentally from my experience with the change projects in businesses, administrations, hospitals, universities, and armies in industrial countries. In these projects, too, I observed a striking discrepancy between the models of "good" organizational change and the reality perceived by project participants. Whereas organizational designers, drawing on compelling concepts such as the learning organization and the knowledge-based company, assume that predictable and controllable change is possible, the actual processes of change are plagued by problems, contradictions, and conflicts.

The explanations that management literature offers for this discrepancy between the noble principles of the models and concepts, on the one hand, and the problems, contradictions, and conflicts, on the other, have certainly left many readers baffled. The literature tends to attribute these difficulties solely to implementation problems. It tends to provide formulas—often with new and attractive-sounding names—to make change processes even more successful through more and better objectives, participation, self-organization, staff motivation, and learning. The names continue to change—yesterday's "change organization" becomes today's "learning organization" becomes tomorrow's "intelligent organization"—but the practical advice for organizational change remains largely the same. Given all the supposedly effective advice, it is astonishing that the participants in change projects still suffer from so many contradictions and dilemmas.

As opposed to this type of management literature, I do not aim in this book to show that the discrepancy between models of "good" organizational change and the intrinsic problems of actual change processes result from the inadequate implementation of the change concepts themselves. Rather, I wish to demonstrate that they result from supposedly rational notions about organizational change. A central insight of systems-theoretical organizational research is that businesses, administrations, armies, hospitals, and universities function only to a very limited degree according to the officially disseminated assumptions about rationality. As a result, this research is focused primarily on the differences between the various departments and teams as well as on the differences between various hierarchical levels. From the perspective of a differentiating approach within systems theory, the contradictions, paradoxes, and dilemmas in organizations are no longer stigmatized as unhealthy conditions, but are understood as integral components of change processes that can be masked only provisionally by fashionable models.

Despite this fundamental skepticism about assumptions of rationality in organizational change, it would be mistaken to conclude that we can dispense with rational-sounding models such as the learning organization altogether. This is where rainmakers come into play. To natural scientists, it is of course perfectly clear that the rainmakers that are widespread in many parts of Africa do not actually make rain. Nevertheless, it would be problematic for traditional cultures to do without them. As anthropologists and sociologists pointed out in the early twentieth century, their usefulness lies not so much in their official mandate to produce rain by supernatural means, but in ensuring the cohesion of village communities. In the engagement with the problem of a lack of rain, rainmakers offer their communities the opportunity to discuss whether the gods and spirits are well disposed toward them. The "rainmaker effect" is based on the following insight: while it is true that many social institutions do not fulfill their explicit promises, they nevertheless have useful functions, even if these are not immediately evident.[1]

The central thesis of this book is that we can observe this type of rainmaker effect in many of the concepts that are being bandied about in management circles today, including that of the learning organization, the knowledge-based company, and the agile system. These relatively new management concepts promise to provide proven, supposedly rational principles for successful organizational change. The assumption behind them is that companies can count on the success of their change projects only if change processes are organized according to tried-and-tested principles, which include clear objectives, employee identification, participation, communication, and continuous learning.[2] This book will fundamentally challenge the soundness of these principles, though without going so far as to claim that these new change-oriented management concepts are completely useless. As with rainmakers, they contain a hidden benefit. They provide employees with orientation in situations of great uncertainty. The principles of good organizational change are no more likely to lead to success-

---

1   In the early twentieth century, sociologist Émile Durkheim (Durkheim 1915) and social anthropologist Bronislaw Malinowski (Manlinowski 1948) examined these latent functions of magic and religious practices. In 1931 Charles A. Bennett described the rainmaker phenomenon in his book *The Dilemma of Religious Knowledge* (see the new edition, Bennett 1969).

2   On management as magic and the search for salvation in reengineering projects, see (Fincham 2000, 174–191).

ful planned change measures than rainmakers are to produce rain. However, in moments of radical upheaval, these principles create and preserve a sense of community in businesses, administrations, and associations—as do rainmakers in African villages.

The Three Sides of an Organization

My examination of concepts such as the learning organization, the knowledge-based company, and the agile system is based on the assumption that one must systematically distinguish between three "sides" of organizations (Kühl 2013, 87ff.). The visible *display side* is the organization's façade. Through decoration, ornament, or even uniformity, this side is intended to represent something (Rottenburg 1996, 191ff.). Organizations present an attractive façade to the outside world in order to appeal to customers, ensure that the media take a positive view of them, or to establish legitimacy with political actors. What goes on in the rear is not entirely unimportant, but the organization's survival is often heavily dependent on the beautification and window dressing up front. The organization's *formal side* is the official set of rules to which its members are bound. This is the aspect of the organization that most strongly calls to mind the workings of a machine. Like machines, organizations consist of precisely defined parts. Each part has a set function within the machinery (Ward 1964, 37ff.). An organization's *informal side* can best be described using the metaphor of a game. When we take a closer look at this side, we may be reminded of the soccer match between the two teams of animals in Walt Disney's *Bedknobs and Broomsticks*. Others have compared the "wild" life of organizations to a game played on a round sloping pitch with a large number of goal posts. The players can throw in extra balls whenever they like and must make sure they get credit for the goals they shoot (Weick 1976, 1).

In my view, the learning organization, the knowledge-based company, the holacratic firm, the agile system, or whatever the concepts of rational organizational change will be called in the future all represent changes to the display side of the organization. Whereas in the past organizations presented mainly rational organizational forms to the public, they are now increasingly praising their supposedly rational forms of organizational change. In this book, I take seriously the visible display side of the learning organization, the knowledge-based company, and the agile system. I attempt to show what would happen if organizations actually lived by the principles that are presented as the rational tenets of change. My thesis is that such principles, which have a persuasive effect when they appear on the display side, yield a variety of unwanted side effects in organizational routines. These side effects may explain why the learning organization and the knowledge-based company never work in the way described when presented on the display side.

The Challenges of Writing an Organizational Studies Book That Is Readable for Organizational Practitioners

When writing this book, I faced the challenge of connecting the problems observed in change projects by organizational practitioners to the findings of organizational research. There are a number of legitimate reasons why communication barriers exist between organizational practice, on the one hand, and organization studies, on the other. Organizational practitioners need to eliminate problems in organizations at short notice and inevitably identify with the solutions they choose. By contrast, organizational researchers are most interested in accurately describing organizations. They often have a highly detached view of organizational problems and their possible solutions.

Despite these communication barriers, I hope that with my contribution to the discussion about the learning organization and the knowledge-based company, I will succeed in bridging the gap between the largely separate worlds of organizational theory (which hardly ever ventures beyond the ivory tower) and organizational practice. Organizational scholars will be required to follow a discussion about ideas and theses in essay form, which may not meet the usual criteria of scholarly discourse. In this essay, which admittedly has grown quite long, I draw on stories from the inner workings of organizations for illustrative purposes, but I do not intend to introduce them with the detailed case reports and methodological explanations common in organizational research. Nevertheless, despite this departure from the usual norms of academe, organizational scholars—assuming they will not be put off by the essayistic character of the text—may discover theses or observations that can be used to advance the academic debate on organizational change.

Let me put organizational practitioners at their ease by emphasizing that this is not a typical scholarly work. Although it is based on a systems-theoretical approach to organizational research, it presents ideas in accessible form. Still, practitioners will be expected to grapple with a perspective on organizations that might go against common ideas about "cohesion" and "promises of success." The reflections in this book are meant to be practical, but they are not meant to be translated directly into action. Anyone who hopes to find a checklist on the last page entitled "What you need to do differently next week" will be disappointed. And anyone who expects to learn sure routes to greater organizational success, financial wealth, and optimal change management should put this book aside.

1.
Introduction: The Limits of the Learning Organization

"The more systematically people proceed,
the more likely they are to fall victim to chance."
Friedrich Dürrenmatt

Organizations that learn a great deal systematically and that manage knowledge effectively are better than organizations that learn very little or nothing at all. This is the commonly accepted assumption behind the learning organization. The more we change, the better we are at adapting to changing environmental conditions. The learning organization is touted as the organizational form that can best respond in a proactive way to changing environmental conditions. It encourages constant learning and the development of individual skills that allow employees and the company as a whole to adapt in flexible ways (Otala 1995). It is the only type of organization that is adept at creating, acquiring, and transferring knowledge, and at modifying its behavior to reflect new knowledge and insights (Garvin 1993). The aim is essentially an organization that learns continuously—which is why cutting-edge scholars and consultants have stopped using the term "learning organizations" and prefer instead to talk of "fast-learning organizations," the "fastest-learning organizations," and even "super-fast-learning organizations."

Many of the characteristics of the learning, the fast-learning, and the fastest-learning organization are currently being presented as crucial success factors for companies, administrations, and associations. These include open communication, self-organization, participation, viewing employees as a key resource, short learning cycles, independent working styles, and trust-based organizational cultures. Proponents of the concept argue that in a "virtuoso mix of methodologies" many of the change management instruments that were previously used separately are now being combined in new ways and systematically expanded in an effort to create comprehensive learning organizations. Among these instruments are benchmarking, quality circles, continuous improvement processes, teamwork, balanced scorecards, and networking.

According to its proponents, the learning organization can square the circle. With its focus on organizational change, it is oriented to customers, innovation, employees, processes, and products all at the same time. It leads only to win-win situations in which the diverse needs of customers, management, stakeholders, and employees are met.[3]

To a greater degree than other concepts, the learning organization brings together the ideas about predictable and controllable change that are currently a dominant theme in management circles. Most of the literature on learning organizations explores how organizations can improve their learning and knowledge management processes and more effectively design change projects. Its aim is to articulate the conditions and instruments that support learning, knowledge acquisition, and knowledge-sharing within organizations. The literature not only analyzes unhealthy learning processes, impediments to change, and defensive routines, but also seeks to develop mechanisms to overcome these problems.

But the literature does not ask whether organizations that learn and manage knowledge effectively actually function better than those that do not. Nor does it question the ideas about controllable change that are communicated by the learning organization model.

---

3   When it comes to this positive view of learning, the comments by practical-minded managers and consultants do not differ substantially from those by the scientifically oriented exponents of action-based learning theory, such as Argyris and Schön. Even the latter argue that sophisticated learning ensures an organization's success and improves working conditions for all employees.

Idealizing the Learning Organization

There are two main reasons why critical examinations of the learning organization concept are so rare. In the first place, the concepts of the learning organization and the knowledge-based company have mobilized a large number of humanist-sounding organizational ideas. Whether it is participation, the focus on people, communication, self-organization, or continuous change, these ideas are so positively charged that any criticism of learning organizations provokes accusations of anti-humanism.

In the second place, the learning organization so far exists only as an ambitious objective. The claim is made that the concept has been implemented only partially in organizational practice. Proponents point out that the organizations that wish to apply the model continue to struggle with delays and difficulties because employees require more time to switch from a hierarchical organization to a continuously changing one. This argument allows supporters to shield the model from one important piece of criticism: failure in practice. If companies, associations, and administrations describe themselves as learning organizations in the making, it is impossible to prove that learning organizations have actually failed. It can always be argued that an organization has failed because it has not learned enough—not, for example, because it has learned too much.[4]

For this reason, one can observe a tendency in various fields of organizational studies to delegate the study of the management concept of the learning organization, the knowledge-based company, and the agile firm to scholars of religion or mythology. To the detached researcher, many of the items on the wish list of "good" organizational change may indeed seem to have more in common with voodoo magic than with fundamental changes in organizational practice.[5] For this reason, many of the scholars who study organizational learning and knowl-

---
4 See, as an example, (Almeida/Soares 2014).
5 See (Clark/Salaman 1996) for one of the first examinations of voodoo magic, organizational witchdoctors, and management rituals. On the learning organization as a management fashion, see also (Jackson 2002, 179ff.)

edge management prefer to concentrate on "real" learning and change processes in organizations instead of engaging more intensely with the new management models oriented toward organizational change.

By contrast, this book focuses on these very management concepts, including that of the learning organization, the evolutionary enterprise, and the knowledge-based company.[6] While it is true that such models of "good" organizational change are linked only loosely to the actual practice of organizational change, this link does exist. In organizations these models shape the thinking and debates on change as a process that can be planned and controlled, and are thus highly influential. Thanks to their direction-giving, meaning-creating, and legitimizing function, they affect the concrete design of change processes as principles of "good" action.

An Ideal-Typical View of a Management Fashion

I would like to take the supporters of the learning organization at their word and examine the criteria for rational organizational change in terms of their viability. In the process, I plan to treat the models of good change management as ideal types. Sociologist Max Weber developed the concept of the ideal type as an investigative method for understanding complex social situations. An ideal type is a (re)construction of a largely rational organizational schema. A coherent model is designed and used as a grid to analyze developmental trends in organizations.

With the help of the ideal-typical learning organization, we can critically question the supposedly rational management concepts that are associated with it: Why are the traditional ideas about a rational organizational structure no longer viable? Why have the management concepts based on organizational structures, such as lean management

---

[6] Despite the focus of this book, I do not completely disregard insights from the sociological and psychological discourse on organizational learning. I aim to address selected aspects of the learning concepts proposed by the action theorists affiliated with Argyris and Schön and the behavioral decision theorists led by Cyert, March and Olsen—though without laying claim to a comprehensive discussion of these theories. On the difference between organizational learning and the learning organization, see (Örtenblad 2001).

and business process reengineering, lost their persuasiveness (Chapter 2)? What is new about the learning organization concept? What role do the rules of good organizational change play in this concept? How are ideas about predictable and controllable change catching on in organizations as a result of this new model (Chapter 3)? What are the weaknesses of the new "ideal" organizational form that is focused on change and learning? How viable are the generally accepted principles of learning organizations such as clear shared objectives, employee identification, participation, self-organization, and change as a continuous learning process? What blind spots do organizations create for themselves when using this management concept (Chapter 4)? If the criteria of learning organizations are not as rational as hoped, what function is performed by promoting this concept? What are its hidden benefits? With learning organizations, are we perhaps confronting a particularly sophisticated strategy that is rooted in irrationality, ignorance, and forgetfulness, but ultimately makes organizations capable of action (Chapter 5)? What do such reflections signify for organizational change in practice? Are there other alternatives to be considered besides such ideas about good organizational change (Chapter 6)?

In studying the weaknesses and hidden benefits of the learning organization model, I hope to provide insight into the processes of organizational change. It is worth noting that many managers recognize the inherent complexity of organizations and have increasingly distanced themselves from the overly simplistic management ideas that long dominated discussions of efficient and effective organizational structures. Nowadays it is quite rare to see organizations being treated like simple machines. The belief in the "one best way" of organization appears to have fallen out of favor (Chapter 2).

On the other hand, relatively simple ideas about rationality and management appear to be slipping in again through the back door. Although managers no longer assume there is *one* good organizational structure, they do believe in the rules of good organizational change. In management and consulting circles, the idea is increasingly taking hold that organizations can develop stable criteria for successful change projects. It is assumed that in a well-planned change process, the participating employees will find effective solutions to the identified problems and put these solutions into action. The learning organization, the evolutionary enterprise, and the knowledge-based company are the management models through which such ideas about rational organizational change are being promoted (Chapter 3).

When change processes run into difficulties, we often hear the excuse that employees have not sufficiently internalized the criteria for good organizational change. It is argued that there have been too little participation, self-organization, communication, and learning; that staff have not yet reached the point where they are able to meet the rational criteria for good organizational change and successfully complete a change project.

This analysis is based on the assumption that organizational change can proceed rationally and effectively if organizations succeed in coming to grips with the human factor. The underlying belief is that the problems can be overcome if the organizational requirements can be adequately aligned with people's hopes and expectations.

I would like to fundamentally challenge this explanation of the problems that arise in the course of change processes. Linking these problems to human beings obstructs the view of the structural difficulties encountered in such processes in companies. It causes experts in organization design to become attached to relatively simplistic assumptions about the controllability and manageability of such processes. Distancing myself from these ideas about controllability, I will focus instead on developing an understanding of organizations that explains and illustrates the conflicts that repeatedly arise in change processes.[7]

My thesis is that models of good organizational change seem plausible only if we are prepared to ignore the fundamental contradictions they contain. The concept of the learning organization and the

---

7   This means that I am abandoning the concept of resistance to change. The use of the term "resistance" suggests that a proper response exists, but another one is chosen due to stupidity, moral scruples, or personal interests. If we assume that the members of an organization face various conflicting demands, it is no longer possible to speak of resistance so indiscriminately. Because proper behavior cannot be clearly defined in such contradictory situations, resistance represents only the limited view of participants who are dissatisfied that their favored approach has not been chosen.

evolutionary enterprise appear rational only if we accept numerous blind spots. An examination of these blind spots reveals that the prescriptions and descriptions of learning organizations—such as clear objectives, employee identification with the organization, the focus on people, self-organization, communication, and continuous learning processes—are highly problematic.[8] If strictly applied, they can even cause an organization to fail. There are good reasons to maintain a healthy skepticism toward current ideas about rational organizational change (for more on this topic, see Chapter 4).

However, my mention of the blind spots of learning organizations should not be construed as a fundamental argument against using this management model. Although the criteria of good organizational change are not as viable as many suggest, the model performs not-so-obvious functions. Often the systematic suppression of the problematic side effects of organizational change is needed for organizations to summon the courage to test new processes in situations of great uncertainty. The model of the learning organization can help organizations to disregard such side effects. It may sound paradoxical, but the strength of the learning organization as a management model lies precisely in such ignorance, irrationality, and amnesia. However, there is a danger that these properties can plunge organizations into serious crises (Chapter 5).

This book fundamentally challenges the ideas about organizational structure, controllability, and manageability that have dominated organizational change agendas. However, it should not be seen as an appeal for a postmodern "anything goes." Nor does it align itself with the growing number of books and articles that attempt to debunk current management concepts as hot air or old wine in new bottles. Rather, it aims to elaborate an overarching approach to change processes that does not force us to become champions of every new rational and optimal model, but which specifically uses this model to make the organization more "ignorant" and thus more capable of action.

---

8 The paradoxical-seeming recognition of blind spots is facilitated by a shift in the observer's perspective. A first-order observer cannot recognize blind spots, while a second-order observer can. However, this observer then produces her own blind spots.

The solution that is promoted in this book is based on the idea that there are two ways to deal with the many contradictions in organizations. The first is to suppress the contradictions with the help of the models described above. The second is to critically question the myths of rationality and confront organizations with their respective blind spots. There are good reasons to choose either one of these two approaches. The art of management increasingly lies in either adequately suppressing or mobilizing the dilemmas, paradoxes, and contradictions associated with a given situation (Chapter 6).

2.
The End of the Dream of the Optimal Organizational Structure

> "The test of a first-rate intelligence is the ability to hold
> two opposing ideas in mind at the same time
> and still retain the ability to function."
>
> F. Scott Fitzgerald

One of the most cherished assumptions in management circles is that in the past, companies, administrations, hospitals, universities, and associations worked in stable environments in which managerial tasks were relatively easy. Management teams could concentrate on designing organizational boundaries that let in clear information from the outside world and kept everything else out. All of the contradictions in the outside world were translated into a few clear messages as they passed through these narrowly defined gateways. Information that caused change was ignored. A deliberate attempt was made to avoid the impression that a matter could be handled differently.

For example, the employees responsible for processing orders focused solely on the customer requests that could be processed without changing organizational routines. All other requests were rejected with comments such as "You've come to the wrong place" or "We don't carry that." It was commonly believed that the organization functioned like a simple machine.

It is of course illusory to think that under stable environmental conditions management can seal off boundaries such that conflicting information cannot enter the organization. Customers might not buy as many cars, toothbrushes, or pots as management planned based on last year's sales figures. Or customers may change their requests at short notice, new investors may be solicited, or employees may attempt to assert their own interests against those of management.[9]

A central challenge for managers is to facilitate both stability and change at the same time. Facing changing environmental conditions, managers need to promote organizational change while simultaneously safeguarding the continuity of value creation and keeping the company's image stable. They must ensure the capacity to change (in order to adapt the organization to changing conditions and cope with unpredictable situations) while guaranteeing a high level of technological and organizational predictability and controllability. To facilitate collective action, they must define the rules, values, and attitudes that are accepted by all employees and, in addition, implement change against the will of the affected groups of workers.

In the first section of this chapter (2.1), I show that in bureaucratic and Taylorist organizational models—as well as in lean management and business process reengineering—the central problem posed by the simultaneity of stability and change is solved by establishing separate organizational responsibilities. Specialized units are tasked with designing value-added activities in stable processes, while other units such as purchasing, sales, and quality assurance are given responsibility for adapting organizations to the new requirements of the exterior world.

However, this separation of functions—innovation and change activities, on the one hand, and stable value-added activities, on the other—has now become increasingly risky. The second part of this chapter (2.2) will show that the separation of innovation activities from routine tasks prevents change from being implemented in a timely fashion. This is why management teams are now calling for all organizational units to pursue innovation and change independently while carrying out routine activities. The difficulty is that these continuous change processes tend to produce greater uncertainty and instability in daily organizational operations (2.3).

---

9   In organizational studies, the basic problem of stability and change is described in various ways. I prefer the opposing colloquial terms "stability" and "change" to the distinctions made in the theoretical literature between "variation" and "retention" (Weick 1979) or "variety" and "redundancy" (Luhmann 2003).

2.1. An Initial Approach to Solving the Dilemma of Stability and Change: Stable Organizational Structures with Change-Oriented Units

Charting a middle course seems the most obvious response to the conflicting requirements of stability and change. For the impartial observer, a happy medium is the easiest way to cope with the problem of change and stability, which require different types of organizational action. Seen superficially, it seems sufficient, as a first step, to determine how much change a social system can bear without jeopardizing its identity or existence, and then to make sure that the organization remains in this state of balance.

Some schools of management liken this balancing act to the "strategy" employed by trees in violent storms. A tree must have the necessary stability—ensured by its root system—to weather the storm. In addition to its stable root system, though, the tree requires a certain degree of flexibility to bend to the force of the storm. If its trunk is too rigid, the tree will fall over.

The danger of this type of comparison is that by simplifying the matter, it obscures a basic paradox. The demand for balance and compromise must not allow us to lose sight of the fundamentally contradictory processes involved in any attempt to promote both innovation and change. A focus on change is at odds with a focus on stability. Change and stability are antithetical for the very reason that every change disrupts the existing order and the existing order impedes any attempt to change.

Change-Oriented Units and a Protected Core

It would be highly problematic for management teams if every instance of uncertainty and every conflicting requirement directly affected the entire organization. It is not hard to imagine the consequences if one small disturbance immediately mobilized an entire team. One bit of information on conflicting requirements could cause everyone in the organization to rack their brains over how to process the contradictions.

If, upon receiving an unusual order, management immediately stopped the assembly line in order to make sure that all members of the workforce could ponder the problem, an efficient work structure would probably never evolve. If, in response to a complaint by a single customer, all of the company's employees immediately interrupted their normal tasks to investigate the cause of the complaint, the organization would probably never complete its actual work.

According to organizational sociologist James D. Thompson, a central strategy long implemented by experts in organization design was to isolate the organization's value-creating productive core from uncertainty and conflicting demands. The value-creating core can, for example, be the assembly line of an automotive supplier, the warehouse and shipping department of a wholesaler, the administrative department of a public authority, or the laboratory of chemical research institute. These value-adding units of companies and public administrations are hermetically sealed off in the sense that they only receive information that is more or less constant.[10]

Management shields this value-creating core by creating functions, structures, and rules designed to eliminate uncertainties and contradictions for the employees working in it. It defines areas of responsibility that are intended to "guarantee" that the productive core works efficiently. Specialists are trained and given the sole task of making sure that the employees in the productive core can perform their work. In other words, management creates departments that are paid to ensure that the value-creating core continues to believe in stable environmental requirements.

For example, the purchasing department of a company, working together with warehousing, makes sure that sufficient supplies of raw

---

10 Thompson's reflections (Thompson 1967) are based on the distinctions described by sociologist Talcott Parsons, who argued that organizations need to fulfill three different functions. The first part of the organization performs the function of production. The second part carries out the managerial tasks of supervising and coordinating organizational activities. The third adapts the organization to the normative requirements of society (see also Scott 1995, 21).

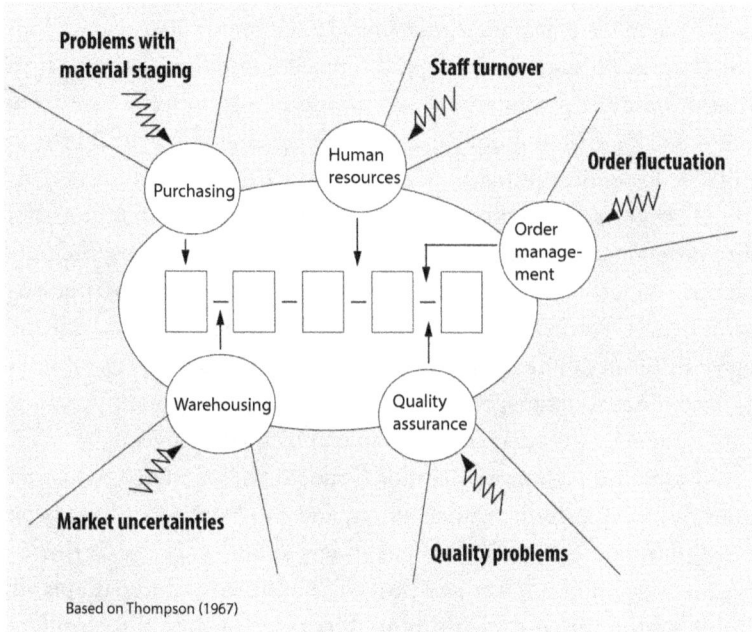

Fig. 1: Protecting against Uncertainty with Buffering Units

materials are always available for production processes. Production planning and management see to it that production is never interrupted. Maintenance is responsible for equipment operating reliably and not breaking down. The job of the reception staff and security personnel is to prevent troublesome disturbances form affecting the production process. The human resources department is responsible for guaranteeing the availability of sufficient staff and smoothly replacing disruptive or potentially disruptive elements. In collaboration with the reworking department, quality assurance improves possible problems in the production process without disrupting production. Working together with shipping, sales is responsible for organizing the sale and delivery of goods such that the produce core is not disturbed, say, by the temporary storage of semi-finished or finished goods on the company's premises.

In addition to functions such as purchasing, quality assurance, maintenance, and sales—all of which directly shield the productive core from market changes (the technical environment)—organizations create rules, functions, and departments (e.g., public relations, legal) that protect the productive core from destabilizing influences from the political, legal, cultural, and scientific spheres and defend it from possible losses of legitimacy (Meyer/Rowan 1977).

These units have a monopoly on changing the organization's rules and programs, but they can do so only to a limited degree. The purchasing department can alter the rules governing the procurement of materials. Production planning and management can override the agreed-on rules (which are often programmed into IT systems) so as to keep the production process running. Personnel can modify recruitment strategies in order to hire more compliant employees.

Ideally, this organizational model functions like a large industrial greenhouse. The gardeners, chemists, and mechanics that have been hired to run the greenhouse are paid solely to buffer against detrimental environmental impacts and provide the lettuce and tomato plants inside with optimal conditions at all times. The goal is to regulate temperatures, sunlight, nutrients, and pests such that the lettuce and tomatoes can grow in an environment in which it is always a sunny 68 degrees Fahrenheit and pests have been eradicated.

Such a comparison provides insight into the frequently lamented paralysis in middle management. The function of middle management is to filter out various environmental requirements so that only clear information reaches the organization's productive core. That this core at times seems paralyzed (because it can perform only narrowly defined actions) is not a failure but intended organizationally.

Ultimately, the organization "buys" the balance between stability and change by growing in size. The productive core is shielded by additional departments that provide it with stable work instructions (Scott 2003). The talk of "bloat," "top-heaviness," and "flab" in organizations is explained by this trend. The explosion in the overhead costs that are allocated to the productive units is the price companies pay for a stable production process.

Taking a somewhat heretical view, we might compare this situation to the role played by the infamous Stasi secret police in former East

Germany. The Stasi protected the state's "productive core" of workers from excessive disruptions. In organizational terms, this was certainly no easy task to pull off. The relatively high salaries of Stasi officers were justified not by their contribution to East Germany's GNP, but by the contribution these officers made to safeguarding productivity. Such a perspective allows us to understand why representatives of the system found it scandalous for members of the civil rights movement to chant "Stasi in die Produktion" ("Stasi to the factories") at their demonstrations. The Stasi was able to perform its protective tasks, which were so crucial for the "organization," for the very reason that its members were not burdened with the work in production.

Single-Loop Learning by Employees in the Productive Core

Like the above-mentioned tomatoes growing in an industrial greenhouse, workers in the value-creating productive core are given the impression that environmental requirements are always constant and clear. However, in cases where environmental turbulences reach this core, they are perceived as a massive disruption for which there is no suitable remedy.

Single-loop learning is all that is expected of workers in this value-creating core. They are hired not to modify rules, but to follow them. They are told that complex thinking is not necessary because others are paid for it. They are expected only to identify and correct deviations from the prescribed rules.

Even the engineer Frederick W. Taylor, who invented "scientific management," assumed that managers could cope with complex markets, supply processes, and production lines only if experts translated environmental uncertainties into manageable and predictable work processes. According to Taylor, workers did not need to know anything about the complexity of markets or work processes. Too much knowledge of the entire process would only distract them from their work.

In terms of its operations, the productive core is comparable to a "trivial" machine. According to Heinz von Foerster, a machine is deemed trivial if a predefined input into this machine leads to the same output.[11] Business owners and managers, in their role as "mechanics," provide an input and fire their machine up. The gears begin turning and the machine produces a precisely defined output. If managers order workers to process paper into 5,000 cardboard boxes, they can assume that 5,000 cardboard boxes will appear at the end of the process as output.

If, contrary to expectations, 5,000 cardboard boxes are not produced, the mechanics assume—following the logic of trivial machines—that there is a problem either with the paper that has been added, the production equipment, or the employees operating the machine. The mechanic attempts to eliminate this problem, and once the input, the production equipment, or the workers have been "repaired," the trivial machine is started up again.

Sociologist George Ritzer (Ritzer 2011, 118) has compared the work in such value-creating cores to the children's game of painting by numbers. Employees receive clear instructions and produce a precisely specified product based on them. They do nothing more than connect the prearranged dots to create a precisely defined picture. In a sense, the work process is "doubled": it exists once as an elaborate managerial plan and once as a real process in which predefined steps are carried out according to this plan. In the logic of this system, employee creativity, originality, and inspiration are only obstacles.

At the Bosch engineering and electronics company, workers in the value-creating productive once described their role with a pithiness typical of their Swabian dialect: "I schaff beim Bosch und halt' mei Gosch'"—"I work at Bosch and shut my trap." Their saying reflects the commonly held view that low-level employees should not think too much on the job because they can rely on salaried employees who are not part of the same time-tracking system to keep contradictory demands or ambiguities from reaching them during work.

The monotony of assembly line work is ultimately the result of this isolation. It arises because surprises and contradictions are not

---

11 For the distinction between trivial and nontrivial machines, see, for example, (Foerster 2003). In contrast to the simplistic visualization of the trivial machine, Foerster used differentiation as an observation perspective.

allowed to penetrate to the productive core. The contradictions are so heavily cushioned that the employees' actions can be defined in detail. It is now possible, for example, to tell workers in an automotive assembly plants that they will be performing the same standardized hand movements every twenty seconds for the next two years. The maids in a luxury hotel can be ordered to perform exactly 104 tasks during the thirty minutes they spend in each room. They know how to position the notepads next to the telephones in the rooms and how to arrange the three sheets of stationery and three envelopes in the information folders. Burger King managers can dictate how workers are to smile to customers, put ice in cola cups, and fold the paper bags containing hamburgers.

As a result, employees in production may hardly notice market changes at all. However, the managers who complain that their employees are not aware of radical market fluctuations and that they therefore tend to undermine their proposals for change are wrong to attribute this behavior to the workforce's ignorance. The employees' limited awareness of the market is due to the fact that they are shielded from market events by a large number of organizational units. In other words, the managers who criticize their staff's limited acceptance of the necessity of change are responsible for it themselves within the framework of the described system. The problem lies not solely in the insufficient dissemination of information, but in the decision by the managers' superiors to create their managerial positions in the first place.

Protecting the productive core from environmental uncertainty can at times lead to a grotesque situation in which employees continue doing their work without noticing the company is on the brink of bankruptcy. Assembly line workers in an automotive plant, maids in a hotel, Burger King staff—all normally take little notice of environmental changes while inside the company. In extreme cases, they may continue doing the work they have done for years on the day the company goes belly up. When they arrive at work for the morning shift, they find the gates shut and learn the CEO has absconded to the Bahamas.

The Rational Organization and the Suppression of Uncertainty

By combining departments and hierarchies and creating rules to stabilize these units, organizations buffer against environmental uncertainties and ultimately induce all the affected parties—the organization itself, its employees, and the outside world—to buy into the myth of a clear purpose and effective approaches. Or to put it more simply, the only reason that anyone can believe that an organization has a clear objective and uses suitable and efficient means to achieve this objective is that the organization regularly intercepts contradictions and uncertainties from the environment. The organizational models that are based on stable structures provide us with vivid examples of this.

James D. Thompson (Thompson 1967) succinctly described an organizational model that functions according to rational principles. In his view, organizations aim to be rational, even though, as open systems, they need to respond sensitively to changing environmental influences. By creating "buffering units" that intercept disruptions from the environment, they are able to establish rational rules in their sealed-off, value-creating cores. Over time the impression arises that the operations in this core function according to clear cause-and-effect principles and are embedded in means-ends relationships.

Drawing on the logic of Taylorism, management could easily convey the impression that there were general principles for a rational organization. Market conditions were assumed to be stable, and relatively clear general conditions could be posited. Managers believed they could read this environment like an open book. Thanks to the assumption of a constant and stable environment, it was possible to create the impression that the whole organization pursued a clearly defined, quasi-natural (or better yet: market-given) objective. If, contrary to expectations, customers went elsewhere or difficulties arose with suppliers, experts in management buffered against the uncertainties.

The hope for a rationally functioning, value-creating core was not abandoned in the streamlined, process-oriented organizations of the late twentieth century. Lean management and business process reengineering promoted the idea that productivity could be doubled and costs

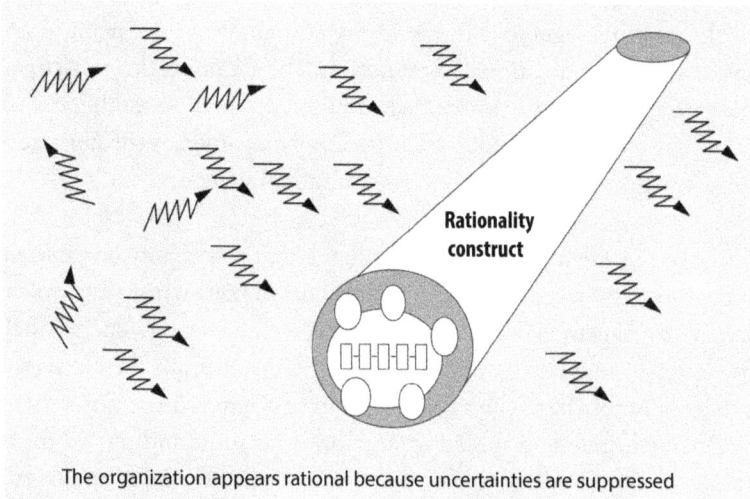

The organization appears rational because uncertainties are suppressed

Fig. 2: Creating the Appearance of Rationality by Suppressing Uncertainty

cut in half if management only reduced the number of hierarchical levels, introduced leaner administrative units, collaborated more closely with suppliers, and organized streamlined value-added processes. These management models emphatically distanced themselves from the idea of a bureaucratic organization in which many tasks were performed in isolation. However, lean management and business process reengineering were also meant to ensure error-free production in a rationally functioning, value-creating core. The difference was that in these new systems, fewer employees worked in the buffering units and the task of buffering against uncertainty was ultimately shifted closer to production. Here the party responsible for mitigating environmental uncertainty was no longer the employee in the individual department, but the "case manager."

Despite all the rhetorical distinctions to Taylorism, the 1990s model of streamlined, process-oriented organizational structures was also presented as the "proper" organizational form because it was the most efficient. And the inventors of lean management and business process reengineering also believed that an optimal organizational form could be found for every market situation. In other words, the proponents of the new management models were still chasing the dream of an optimally adapted, rational organization. The slimming down of organizations, the introduction of decentralized production modules, and the focus on business processes were simply regarded as the next step on the path to an optimal new organizational structure.

However, in the final analysis, we can see that it was only possible to present the above-mentioned organizational models—from Taylorism to lean management to business process reengineering—as rational because unpredictability had first been eliminated from the organization's core processes. The organization either ignored the unpredictability or shifted it to special change-oriented units and settled for a value-creating productive core that was oriented toward rational criteria. In such cases, organizational rationality is ultimately an empty concept that is based simply on a distancing from all that is not rational. This can be seen in the following examples:

Taylorism: Taylor's "scientific management" was based on the assumption that an optimal, scientifically based organizational structure could be derived for every company. However, to create this optimal organizational structure, market fluctuations had to be ignored. The suppression of uncertainty is embodied in the famous statement by American automobile magnate Henry Ford that customers could have his versatile Tin Lizzy in any color they wanted, "so long as it's black." It was possible to portray the mass production of automobiles on an assembly line as a scientific production method only because customer needs and market fluctuations were systematically ignored. It was simply assumed that sales of the Model T would continue to increase as in the past.

Lean management: The only reason the slimmed-down company could be touted as a rational and optimal enterprise was that all the problematic aspects of this strategy were suppressed. One point that has long been ignored is that the potential for innovation is lost when organizational "padding" is reduced. The proponents of lean management refuse to acknowledge that companies require organizational reserves to meet the adaptive requirements arising from constantly changing environmental conditions. In the end, many of the companies that pursued this strategy ended up with rationalized production processes, but no resources with which they could adjust to market changes.

Business process reengineering: It was only possible to present business process reengineering as a rational and coherent management strategy because people accepted its blind spots. What they overlooked was that any attempt to redesign organizations on the drawing board inevitably led to massive resistance within the organization. They also ignored the fact that rethinking and redesigning organizations "from scratch" created an organizational state that while stable became an impediment to much-needed responses to environmental change.[12]

If new ideas about optimal organizational structures emerge in the coming years, it will no doubt be possible to analyze them in the same way. In all these models, the appearance of rationality and superiority is a result of the systematic suppression of potential uncertainties.

Moving from One Rational Organizational Structure to the Next

The basic framework of the management discussion, which built on these assumptions about rationality, was relatively simple for a long time. Participants addressed a variety of supposedly optimal organizational models while ignoring their problems, blind spots, and omissions. These problems and omissions did not become a focus of attention until people began doubting the value of each model.

The usual course of events is as follows: A promising new organizational model—one that is rational and optimized for its environment—is promoted in the press, in books, and at seminars and conferences. It is suggested that with this model, organizations can finally get things "right." A large number of companies, administrations, hospitals, universities, and

---

[12] On reengineering, see Søren Peter Gunge's highly informative essay (Gunge 2000).

associations then use the model in their own reorganization processes. Not only do consulting firms refine the model, but they outdo each other in applying the latest version. No longer content with lean management, they now promote the "hyper lean model"; the "continuous improvement process" (CIP) becomes an even more powerful CIP2 or CIP3. These word creations are trademarked in the belief that they create value.

Once the rational organizational model catches on—either in its original or refined form—it is initially so shielded and protected by praise, stories of success, and how-to formulas that any fundamental criticism is viewed as heresy. Anyone who in this initial phase dares to point out the blind spots of the new, rationally appearing organizational model is ignored or discriminated against. However, the model eventually grows old and no longer seems so original. The initial exuberant hopes are dashed and weak points become evident. Although a few consultants and managers may try to keep the fad alive with books like "The Right Way to Implement Lean Management" or "Common Mistakes in Reengineering," the model has lost its luster.

At this point it is easy to voice criticism. The uncertainties that were ignored so that the model could be presented as rational are now emphasized. The blind spots are interpreted. All of a sudden, the weaknesses of ready-made concepts such as Taylorism, lean management, and business process reengineering are enumerated and discussed. Critics point out that the (now old) organizational model does not meet changed environmental conditions. The rapidly aging concept is dropped and replaced by a new, more persuasive, and more effective one.

In the book *Organizations—A Quantum View* (Miller/Friesen 1984, 202–247), economists Danny Miller and Peter H. Friesen describe how organizations jump from one rational organizational structure to the next. Over longer periods of time, organizations follow clear strategies in a stable environment and base all their operations on these strategies. According to Miller and Friesen, organizational structures, management processes, and employees are coordinated within this framework, and only incremental changes are made. Then "strategic revolutions" take place at regular intervals in which the old organizational structure is replaced by a newer, more rational one.

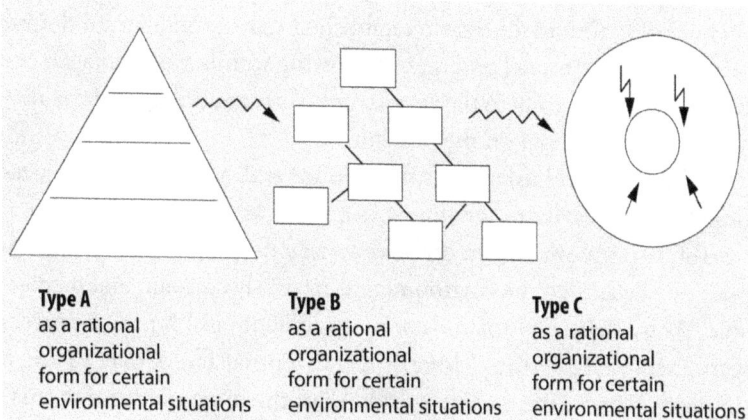

Type A
as a rational organizational form for certain environmental situations

Type B
as a rational organizational form for certain environmental situations

Type C
as a rational organizational form for certain environmental situations

Fig. 3: The Quantum Theory of Organizational Change—Moving from One Optimal Organizational Form to the Next

Managers, consultants, authors, business journalists, and conference organizers expend a great deal of time and energy surfing these management waves. It is crucial to ride the crest of the wave for as long as possible in order to extract as much energy from it as possible. These individuals can try to extend these waves in order to continue reaping benefits, but at some point it is wise for them to step off and catch another wave before they crash over the rocks on the shore.

Often we encounter the paradoxical situation that the very same managers, consultants, and business journalists who long surfed the wave of one particular management fad become its biggest critics once they hop off.

2.2. The Problem with the Optimal Organizational Structure—Sealed-Off Cores

It has now become increasingly clear that this system of constantly changing models of rational organizational design is overheating. The lifespan of each model is becoming shorter. No sooner has a rational organizational model become established than fundamental doubts arise and a new model emerges. A growing number of managers are responding skeptically to the appearance of yet another promising new organizational model on the horizon.

What is behind this trend? Why do ideas about rational organizational structures disappear almost as quickly as they emerge?

The assumption that an organizational structure is optimal presupposes the belief that the environment is relatively constant and predictable. As models, Taylorism, lean management, and business process reengineering function primarily as perceptual filters that ensure a simplistic view of the outside world. All of the minor and major organizational tools linked to these management models, such as position and process descriptions, hierarchies, and departmental systems, are parts of this filter (Luhmann 1973, 182).

Isolated from the Environment

Some organizations are so perfectly cushioned against contradictory information that they no longer perceive environmental changes. Due to the routine nature of their processes, they take in information only selectively. Unusual data that might conflict with their routines is ignored because it is not possible to perceive it in the first place (Crozier 1961, 41–42).

The employees in the effectively sealed-off value-creating cores do not feel responsible for paying attention to information not specified in their work routines—and they are certainly justified in taking this stance. If during the course of the day five customers ask for chili sauce on their hamburgers at a McDonald's restaurant, the employees will probably not regard these unusual customer requests as potentially valuable information. They will not call McDonald's headquarters to inform product developers of a new customer need. Workers on an automotive assembly line are highly skilled at installing precisely defined components, but they are probably unaware of the ways this component could be optimized. Even if they were to recognize them, they would probably not make an effort to initiate the necessary processes.[13]

Because decision-making authority is assigned to managers through organizational programs, the idea of modifying these programs does not occur to workers in the value-creating productive core. They do not consider it their responsibility to look for errors in the program or to consider possible new programs (Luhmann 1968, 338). Comments such as "It's not my job to bother with changes like that" or "I'm here to do what I've been told to do" are the logical consequence of the separation between workers and managers.

Expressed in more radical terms, if employees in this type of traditional organization become aware of information for which no routines exist and then draw conclusions from this information, they are taking a substantial risk. Detailed job descriptions, quality manuals, business processes, plans, and work instructions clearly define what is expected of each employee and also let employees know what is not expected of them. Those who wish to change generally accepted, existing routines because they believe they have recognized a changed environmental condition run the risk of disrupting the prevailing organizational consensus. By spoiling the carefully established game, they also risk being excluded as troublemakers.

A few cynical observers have noted that bureaucratic companies function like the politburos of former communist states. When these states still existed, the only information that the politburo members gave credence to was that which fit into their worldviews and could be interpreted as an additional step on the road to socialism's final victory. Anyone who offered a divergent opinion was branded a dissident and banished along with the information they offered.

---

13 Employee suggestion programs and continuous improvement processes can be seen as attempts by management to use cash and other incentives to get employees to feel enthusiastic about tasks that these employees used to perform before the productive core was sealed off.

Self-Affirmation Loops

In some cases, bureaucratic organizations develop true self-affirmation loops. An organization's rigid structures and strict rules can cause its members to perceive only a highly limited cross-section of their environment. These rigid structures act like filters that let in only compatible information. Of course, this process strengthens the conviction that the organization's current structure is completely right. Structures and rules become further entrenched and the filter becomes further refined. The result is a self-reinforcing process in which the organization repeatedly grasps the environment as confirming its mechanisms, although this environment is perceived only from the organization's limited perspective.

The Swedish company Facit provides a good example of how this self-affirmation loop works (Starbuck 1983). In the 1970s Facit was one of the leading manufacturers of mechanical calculators, typewriters, computers, and office furniture. Management regarded the production of mechanical calculators as the company's core competency and concentrated mainly on the mechanical calculator market. Facit invested large sums of money in building new factories and expanding customer service and was able to manufacture high-quality mechanical calculators at a very low price. Suddenly, though, it lost one major customer after the other. What happened? Management had focused the entire organization on a single successful product. The sales offices only saw developments in the market for mechanical calculators and management took the demand there as justifying a further expansion of this core business. The entire company was trapped in a clear self-affirmation loop that resulted in its not being able to recognize the growing demand for computers as a rival product. Facit had no system in place to collect information linked to changes in the market for electronic calculators.

IBM, the former leader of the U.S. computer industry, is an additional revealing example of this process of circular self-affirmation. In the 1970s and 1980s IBM managers saw mainframe computers as their primary market and directed marketing and sales efforts to the

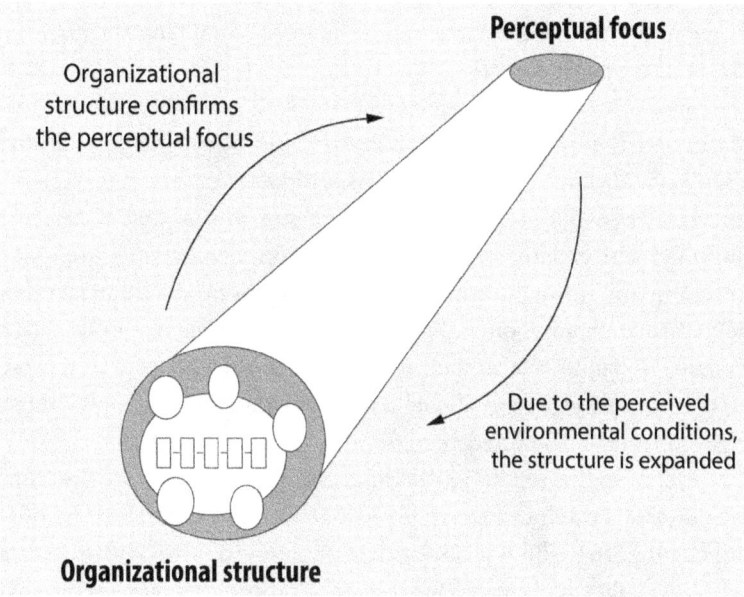

Fig. 4: Self-Affirmation Loop

corresponding customer groups. In other words, staff in the mainframe-based sales structures only perceived information from mainframe customers and regarded it as confirming this approach. As a result, the company furthered optimized its organizational structures for mainframe sales, which in turn focused the company more heavily on mainframe customers. Due to this fixation, IBM management recognized much later than other market participants that its share of the market for personal computers was declining.

A similar process took place in the American automobile industry. Because the sales and marketing structures of the three major U.S. car companies were concentrated primarily on the American market, these companies recognized the demand primarily for large gas-guzzling cars. This perception led them to further expand the corporate structures that were oriented toward the sale of large sedans. As a result, they registered only the customer requests for large sedans and further expanded sales networks for this type of car. In the end, the three major U.S. carmakers had difficulty recognizing the growing demand for compact cars.

In all three cases, management teams had sophisticated information systems in place that they believed could be used to compile and map key data concerning new orders, productivity, and customer satisfaction. Like pilots in a cockpit, they assumed that they were being supplied with reliable information that would enable them to guide the company through turbulent times. They overlooked the fact that self-affirmation loops often slipped into these management information systems unbeknownst to their users and that these loops served more to confirm management's belief that it was always on the right course than to reveal unexpected changes.

Interestingly enough, in the three cases described above, the companies were convinced that they had adapted efficiently to the outside world. They did not notice that they had in fact conformed to a worldview they had created for themselves through their own internal organizational structures. They did not wish to admit that despite all the conferences with customers, market observation systems, and trend-spotting programs, it was a matter of organizational self-adaptation (Weick 1977; Nystrom/Starbuck 1984).

The metaphor that management literature usually uses to describe such self-affirmation loops is that of the frog in the saucepan. As many management books and articles point out, it is impossible to cook a frog by putting it in hot water. Alerted to the cook's intentions by the sudden difference in temperature, the frog will simply hop out of the pan. However, the frog faces a problem if it is placed in cold water that is then slowly heated on the range. The frog will fail to notice the danger and be slowly cooked to death. What is often overlooked when this metaphor is used, though, is that there is no sneaky cook in the real world. The "frog" hops into the saucepan itself and is quite content to allow the temperature to rise. The frog thinks that the hotter water is increasing its well-being and even accelerates the process. It fails to see that the long-term rise in temperature is not beneficial at all.

One of the great illusions in the management discussion in recent years is that this problem can be avoided with the help of modern, stability-based organizational structures à la lean management or business process reengineering. It has become increasingly clear that the organizations that embrace the ideal of lean management or business process reengineering greatly resemble the frog in the saucepan. Due to their slimming down or their orientation toward business processes, they run the risk of creating a highly efficient self-affirmation loop.

In the lean management model, all organizational resources are pooled and all organizational units are focused on the central value-added process. As a result, these organizational units are unlikely to have the time and energy to register unusual developments. All the members of the organization are concentrated on making the organization more efficient and streamlined. They may no longer notice that while their processes are more efficient, they are unfortunately unable to sell their efficiently produced goods.

In business process reengineering, company processes are reorganized "from scratch" taking the customer's perspective into account. Indirect routes are eliminated. Companies ideally focus their processes on customers and as a result are hardly able to develop products that do not provide a specified customer benefit. Companies are able to optimally adapt to existing customers at short notice, but are unable to recognize newly arising possibilities.

The Myth of Clear Goals

This functional "self-deception" fools management teams into believing that they can rally the organization behind a single goal or a single purpose that dominates everything else. Because of these self-created perceptual limitations, the organization firmly believes that its markets, competitors, and regulatory environment are stable and predictable. As a result, it aligns the entire staff with one goal or purpose. The widespread belief that organizations can pursue objectives and efficiently concentrate their processes and departments on these goals results from this self-deception.

The numerous "management by" concepts in organizations are a result of the belief that there are goals and purposes that can be clearly derived from the environment. The hopes that are pinned on *management by objectives*, *management by inspiration*, and even *management by love* stem from the idea that an organization can achieve its defined goals and purposes by using simple management principles.

Self-affirmation loops do not pose a problem for organizations as long as environmental conditions and real-world prospects do not differ from the organization's own futures plans. To a certain extent, they are even functional. In periods of easy predictability, self-affirmation loops can contribute to a company's success because the logic of the loop can effectively eliminate critical voices, opposition, and difficult employees.

But what happens when the future becomes less predictable?

2.3. The End of the Hope for an Optimal Organizational Structure— Confronting a Turbulent Environment

The future, wrote science fiction writer Arthur Clarke, is no longer what it used to be. In other words, it is virtually impossible to make meaningful statements about what the future will be like. The successes we enjoyed yesterday provide no security for tomorrow. Our assumptions about future developments are undermined by surprises, discontinuities, and instabilities. Despite increasingly sophisticated forecasting tools, matters usually turn out quite differently from the assumptions made in companies, administrations, and associations. According to the philosopher Søren Aabye Kierkegaard, the tragedy of human life is that it can only be understood backwards, but it must be lived forwards. No doubt the same is true of organizations.[14]

Organizations regard a state of affairs as "turbulent" in which they are increasingly confronted with conflicting demands and forced

---

14 The collection of aphorisms on the future is based on (Kets de Vries 1995).

nonetheless to make reasonably reliable predictions about the future. Whereas organizations used to be able to cope with conflicting sets of environmental requirements by choosing one set of requirements over the other, they are now compelled to accommodate both. Prominent examples of conflicting requirements include globalization/localization, quality/price, and competition/cooperation:

Globalization/localization: In the past, companies tended to face the decision of whether to sell standardized products on the mass global market or to serve local niche markets. They could either operate globally with these standard products or confine themselves to specialized, customer-specific products on local markets. Nowadays a growing number of companies are facing the conflicting demands of acting both globally *and* locally. It is becoming increasingly clear that the globalization of market presences is usually accompanied by localization. Ulrich Beck (Beck 2000) has pointed out that no company can produce and market its products globally in the true sense of the word. Maintaining a global presence means being in several places at the same time. Companies that produce, market, and sell products globally must establish production sites locally and tailor goods to the particularities of local markets. The slogan "Think globally, act locally," which was borrowed from the environmental movement, was helpful to companies only for a short time. Now a growing number of organizations must meet the challenge of having to think and act both globally and locally.

Multinational corporations such as Unilever now describe themselves as "multilocal" companies. They have learned, for example, that the Japanese buy very little margarine because they prefer rice to bread and margarine and rice do not go well together. Instead of producing and selling the same successful products in all countries around the world, such globally operating corporations are increasingly adapting to regional particularities. Their objective is to combine a global strategy for product development, production, and marketing with a local adaptation process.

The need for companies to act both globally and locally can lead to paradoxical situations. For the Americans who vehemently demanded an import ban on Japanese cars in the 1980s—because Japanese imports destroyed "American jobs"—the world has surely become a bewildering place. Should they now protest in front of a Mitsubishi car dealership, despite the fact that it invests and owns plants in the U.S.? Or should they demonstrate in front of General Motors outlets because GM has outsourced U.S. jobs to low-wage countries on a massive scale? When company groups combine globalization and localization strategies, consumers' traditional ideas about who is the enemy can be turned on their head.

Quality/price: Companies used to be able to choose between quality and price as key success factors. However, this either-or decision has now evolved into one involving a little bit of both. Companies are increasingly being forced to ensure customer satisfaction by meeting customer-specific quality requirements, while also reducing unit costs through the production of large quantities of goods. Companies need to fulfill the seemingly contradictory goal of offering low prices while ensuring high customer satisfaction through quality and specificity.

For example, as a result of the cut-throat competition among supermarket chains, high-quality products that used to be sold at high prices are now being offered at highly competitive prices. In the past, many supermarket chains could get away with significant price differences between premium and low-quality goods, but they are now facing growing price pressure on premium products—and quality pressure on inexpensive products.

Competition/cooperation: The traditional friend/enemy mentality in many companies no longer works. The only companies that can afford to tell customers who switch to the competition that through this breach of trust they are now their enemies are quasi-monopolists such as Microsoft. It used to be possible to view another business either as a cooperative ally or a competitor, but now many companies must come to grips with a much more complex situation in which worsening competition is requiring greater cooperation. For this reason, they are working with rivals in areas such as research and development while competing with the same companies when it comes to selling of the jointly developed products. They are coming to resemble what journalist Vance Packard calls "cooperative tigers"—predatory animals that achieve their full potential by working with potential or real competitors.[15]

Organizational consultants have written passionate accounts of the successes of companies that have been forced to cooperate with their fiercest rivals in specific fields. One example is Volkswagen and the Ford Group, which formed a strategic alliance to develop and produce a minivan, but then competed when marketing the developed car. The minivan, which was jointly built in a plant to the south of Lisbon, was sold by Ford under the name Galaxy and by VW under the name Sharan.

Or they tell the story of the Lane Group, a British trucking company that supplies highly trained personnel to its competitors. The Lane Group established its own temporary employment agency called PL Workforce because truck drivers from the established temp agencies did not meet its high quality standards. The original purpose of PL Workforce was to supply trained truck drivers to the Lane Group on a temporary basis whenever one of its permanently employed drivers was unable to work due to illness. But PL Workforce increasingly evolved into a business that hired out drivers to competitors on the transport market—a strategy that led to substantial growth.[16]

The need to fulfill conflicting requirements finds expression in a number of paradoxical-sounding neologisms. The terms "global localization" and "glocal" signal the pressure many companies feel to act as global producers and providers of goods while adapting to local conditions. Paradoxical phrases such as "customized mass production" and "mass customization" express the necessity of reducing costs by means of mass production while simultaneously responding to specific customer needs. "Competing cooperation" and "cooptation"—the latter a portmanteau of "competition" and "cooperation"—reflect the pressure many companies are under to cooperate and compete at the same time.

---

15 For example, Packard in one of his many books (Packard 1962, 125).
16 This story can be found in a variety of management books. See, e.g., (Peters 1994, 136).

Given these conflicting requirements, the tried-and-true mechanisms used by organizations to acquire some peace of mind have become prone to failure. A growing number of organizations are facing the problem that due to the increase in unexpected events, discontinuities, and instabilities, their proven rituals of analysis, diagnosis, and planning are no longer effective. They are realizing that their previous methods have placed them on extremely thin ice. The more an organization analyzes, diagnoses, plans, and makes preparations for the future, the more painfully it is struck by reality.

The Tragedy of Structures—the Risk of Crisis

When market or political requirements undergo radical, rapid change, the stable organizational relationships that are created by routines and restrictive mechanisms pose fundamental risks. The paradoxical tragedy of organizational structures and routines is that while the related restrictions facilitate the desired actions, they simultaneously limit horizons. The problem is that structures create the capacity for change in other areas, but are themselves inflexible. Stable structures are an inexpensive way to meet the world's diverse needs, but stability always involves the risk that myriad opportunities will be overlooked.

If the stories we hear from organizations can be believed, the adaptive efforts by the buffering units enclosing the productive core are having difficulty keeping up with the increasingly rapid environmental changes. No sooner is the modification of a program painstakingly introduced and communicated to the technical core than the organization discovers that the newly emerging environmental changes require a new structure. Existing routines are often examined only when a keenly felt crisis occurs (Luhmann 1968, 337). Just before dying, the frog notices that it is no longer in a soothing bath, but is being boiled to death, at which point it often lacks the strength to jump out of the pan.

This type of crisis is not an environmental event that—as is often suggested by management—descends upon the organization from out the blue. Ultimately, it is produced by the organization itself. It arises from the suddenly materializing effects of suppression and ignorance. The better the organization's rational structure, the more the organization suppresses uncertainty and the greater the risk that side effects will build and suddenly emerge in the form of a crisis. At some point the economic pressure from the environment becomes so strong that the organization can no longer ignore it. Often the crisis that then occurs is so acute that it cannot be managed.

The sudden occurrence of crises is familiar to many organizations with highly developed management information and early warning systems. Abruptly and without warning, the instruments and gauges in the managerial "cockpit" that long confirmed that the organization was on the right course soar into the red. Developments have been taking place in the organization's blind spots that have either gone undetected or that have been registered incorrectly by the instruments and early warning systems. Now they come crashing down on the workforce. In such situations, is difficult to respond to changes that occur so suddenly and in such concentrated form.

The Impact of Contradictions

As a result, organizations are increasingly coming under pressure to view environmental changes not only as disturbances of their stable productive cores, but also as opportunities for fundamental change. In other words, they are allowing environmental influences to enter the organization unfiltered. They are mapping out the conflicting requirements internally. Ambiguity, ambivalence, and a lack of clarity are no longer being construed as uncertainties with which the entire organization is confronted—or from which the productive core, at the very least, must be protected—but as opportunities to develop new views, emphases, and definitions.

It is above all the companies operating in turbulent markets that are currently losing their ability to use organizational or temporal separations to buffer against the contradictions between the requirements of stability and change. Fewer companies believe they can address this problem by means of a strict organizational separation between uncertainty- and stability-oriented units or through a phase-based model along the lines of "change in January and February, stability for the rest of the year." At first glance, it seems as though the option available to them is to view the organizational dilemma of change and stability as a personnel problem.

These developments have led to a sudden increase in the number of contradictions and conflicting goals perceived by workers in the value-creating organizational units. Their friendly colleagues from middle management are now no longer able to cushion against the diverse ambiguities and uncertainties from the outside world, which reach the workers in the productive core with much greater frequency. As a result, it is these workers in the productive who must now determine how they wish to cope with order fluctuations, stricter quality requirements, material procurement problems, and so on. They are being asked to view uncertainty not as a lamentable state, but as an inducement to change.

Doubts about Rationality

Regardless of whether managers ever truly believed they could collect enough information to read the environment like an open book, the increase in conflicting demands since the turn of the twenty-first century has provided grounds to doubt this view (Alvesson/Thompson 2005). The criticism of lean management and business process reengineering that began in the 1990s reflected a crisis affecting all of the management concepts that merely offered new rational organizational structures. At the heart of this criticism was the complaint that lean management and reengineering projects either did not achieve their goals or that they achieved them at the expense of undesirable side effects. Management journals and consulting books reported that the majority of change projects did not bring the desired benefits and results.

Even today, most employees—whether at companies, administrations, hospitals, universities, or associations—have experienced discontinued, temporarily interrupted, or half-heartedly completed change processes. Efforts to establish new organizational structures are often accompanied by delays, setbacks, and contradictory demands. Many measures that are introduced with great enthusiasm fail and are silently shelved not long afterward.

Rational action may generally have been possible in a period when the general decision-making framework seemed stable, decision makers were not yet changing along with the environment upon which they depended, and the decisions themselves did not influence organizational goals. But in times of rapidly changing markets, worsening global competition, and fundamental technological upheaval, what manager can claim to work under conditions as comfortable as those?

When the circumstances underlying decisions undergo rapid change, it becomes ever more difficult for organizations to present a rational-seeming structure. The greater the indeterminacy of the environmental information that reaches organizations, the smaller the number of supposedly correct organizational rules that can be activated by interacting with this input (Scott 2003). The thesis of a rational organizational structure now seems increasingly antiquated. In view of the growing contradictions now facing organizations, the models for optimal, rational organizational structures are threatening to vanish.

But experience has shown that when proven ideas about rationality erode, new and more flexible approaches tend to take their place. From the shattered belief in optimal, rational organizational structures there has emerged a new rationality concept that appears to better fulfill the new requirements. The next chapter will take a closer look at one of them.

3.
The Learning Organization and the Hope For "Good" Rules of Change

"If you are given two contradictory instructions, carry out both."
Anyonymous

Even the scholars and managers who previously promoted fashionable concepts such as business process reengineering and lean management are now championing organizational forms that are so flexible, so adaptable, and so versatile that it is hardly possible to say what their specific characteristics are. At the start of the twenty-first century, the relatively static management concepts of the late twentieth century—such as business process reengineering and lean management—have increasingly been supplanted by management models such as the learning organization and the knowledge-based company that center on the organization's capacity for change and innovation.

Taken to its logical conclusion, this one-sided focus on transformation and change leads only to a "chaotic organization." If these models were ever systematically implemented, characteristics such as identity and integration, which are normally created by clear organizational structures, would be lost. Due to the uncompromising focus on change, organizations would no longer be able to develop a sense of unity. In extreme cases, chronic flexibility would destroy the organizational identity. Continuous change produces such great uncertainty that a shared direction for action and shared goals no longer exist.

If, as part of a mass mobilization for change, an organization were to attempt to activate various relations and connections all at the same time, it would lead to a devastating overload. Signals from the outside world would not be intercepted by proven routines, rules, and structures. They would cause immense inner-organizational disruptions.

Every impulse from the organization's environment would trigger spontaneous new improvisation processes. "Meetingitis" would break out and employees would spend all their time in group or project meetings developing new responses.

Drawing on the work of Kurt Lewin, the founding father of organizational development, organizational theorist Karl Weick (Weick 1979) described change-oriented organizations as "chronically unfrozen" systems. After unfreezing their existing structures, such organizations are unable to "refreeze" the new structures. They are in a state of constant agitation since none of their processes can proceed in an orderly fashion. Everything appears to be problematic because past experiences are perceived as risky and there is no longer any faith in clarity.

In critical situations, the constant establishment of new structures can destabilize an organization to such a degree that no collective action is possible. So many changes can be made to a social system that it eventually collapses under the weight of what is perceived to be a massive disruption. Organizations run the risk of disintegrating into a large number of disconnected decisions.

How do the models of the learning organization, the knowledge-based company, and the evolutionary enterprise respond to the threat of self-disintegration that results from change and innovation? What new relationship emerges between stability and change? How can organizations in a state of flux and transition create predictability?

The first section of this chapter (3.1) focuses on a new strategy for resolving the paradox connected to the simultaneous orientation toward stability and change. Organizations no longer create stability only through sound organizational structures, but also through reliable rules for "good" organizational change. The concepts of the learning organization, the knowledge-based company, and the evolutionary enterprise are merely code words for these principles of stable, predictable organizational change.

As I go on to argue in the second section of this chapter (3.2), these concepts point to a new understanding of organizational rationality. In the place of the hope for the "good" or the "proper" organizational structure, the idea is catching on that there are many enduring, proven principles of good organizational change. The assumption that organizations are rational is increasingly yielding to the plausible idea of rationally controllable organizational change (3.3).

3.1. The Learning Organization—New Methods for Resolving the Dilemma of Stability and Change

Many twenty-first-century organizations appear to have made an important realization: the hope for an optimal organizational structure is not very realistic because the future is both uncertain and indeterminable. Forecasting is nothing more than intelligent speculation. For this reason, the goal must be to make organizations as adaptable as possible so that they can respond rapidly to environmental changes.

The Stability of Change

Contrary to what has been suggested in management literature, organizations have not responded to the growing uncertainty by abandoning the principle of stability and predictability and by embracing the principle of transformation and change. The new models have little to do with "chronically unfrozen" organizations. Rather, an attempt has been made to integrate stabilizing factors into change processes. The focus is increasingly shifting to the development of viable principles, rules, and formulas for managing the great variety of challenges. The goal here is apparently to develop principles that "properly master" change.

In a nutshell, this means that there are fewer rational blueprints for how organizations function and a larger number of rational blueprints for how organizations can be changed. The focus is no longer on the rational rule-based nature of structures, but on the rational rule-based design of change. The basis of rational organizational action is no longer "How do we produce?" but "How do we change?"

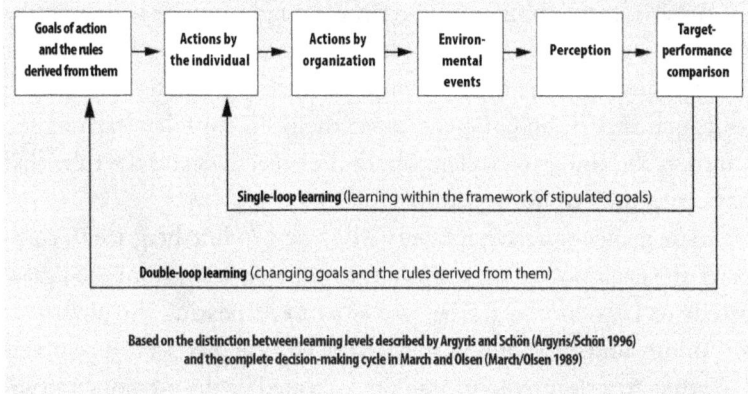

Fig. 5: Simple Single-Loop Learning and Complex Double-Loop Learning

As a result, there is a tendency among organizations to promise employees a new kind of stability. Managers guarantee stable rules for change processes in order to provide the workforce with a minimum degree of stability. Their motto appears to be: we are no longer able to offer employees optimal organizational structures and cannot eliminate the contradictory organizational requirement of having to accommodate both stability and change at the same time. However, we are at least attempting to design the change processes in a predicable way. In other words, employees are to be given a degree of certainty about the rules of change.

Various management philosophies, each with its own descriptive system, have attempted to get a better grasp of this phenomenon. For example, organizational psychologists Chris Argyris and Donald Schön (Argyris/Schön 1978,1996) define it as the transition from simple single-loop learning to complex double-loop learning. In single-loop learning, divergences from the norm are detected and corrected within the framework of existing structures and rules. Employees observe how the environment responds to organizational actions and then carry out target/performance comparisons on the basis of specified goals. In complex or double-loop learning, fundamental objectives and structures are called into question. The basic assumptions that guide action are challenged and modified.

Argyris and Schön compare simple single-loop learning to the functional principle of a thermostat in a house. A thermostat detects divergences from the desired temperature and regulates the heating unit such that it can compensate for them. In complex learning, by contrast, the aim is to challenge both the objectives and the rules that have been derived from them.

Management researcher Henry Mintzberg (Mintzberg 1989) compares the evolution of organizations to the transition from the jigsaw puzzle to Lego bricks. In the case of a puzzle bearing the picture of an Alpine landscape or a Disney character, the pieces are assembled according to a clear pattern. Stability is created by the prescribed structure. In the case of Lego bricks, this prescribed structure no longer exists. Whether the bricks are assembled into an elaborate spaceship or a pink-spotted green dinosaur is determined by the mostly young players. Nevertheless, despite these greater creative freedoms, stability also exists with Lego. It is based on the fact that Lego bricks cannot be assembled randomly. The studs on each brick provide stable building rules: the bricks can be attached only in a straight line or at a right angle. Given the fact that six eight-stud Lego bricks can be combined in a total 102,981,500 ways, this stability is really quite impressive.

The writer Tom Sharpe (Sharpe 1976) makes a similar point. In his cynical analysis of the British education system, he writes that organizational processes function like a gyroscope. A person cannot control in what direction the gyroscope moves on a surface because the effects that this surface has on its movements are far too unpredictable. Nevertheless, the gyroscope is not an unstable entity. Its stability results from the fact that physical laws keep it from falling over while it spins. Likewise, although there is no certainty about the direction change will take, there is certainty about the rules governing the process of change.

In the United States, where it is popular for management philosophies to have esoteric underpinnings, the shift in organizational models has prompted talk of a historical turning point. New Age management theory has proclaimed the dawn of a new era of change. Static "Second Wave" management thinking, which can still be observed at most European and U.S. business schools, is being replaced by "Third Wave" management theory. The categories of linearity and balance are being replaced by the categories of dynamism and change.[17]

Ultimately, managers are merely taking to hear the slogan that "change is the only stable element in our organization"—not in the sense that the organization has disappeared behind all the change, but in the sense that change processes are characterized by a certain reliability regarding expectations.

Code Words for the Principles of Good Organizational Change

How can organizations create stability in their change processes? The rule is simple: companies and administrations must create a set of rules detailing how change should take place within the organization. These fixed rules of change are often found in "change management charters" and publications dealing with the basic principles of organizational change and the disciplines of system thinking and change. Such charters, basic principles, and disciplines all focus attention not only on how an organization should be structured, but on how change needs to take place within it. Instead of rules for the "how" of organization, we now have proposals for the "how" of organizational change.

Change-oriented management models such as the learning organization, the intelligent company, the knowledge-based system, the progressive organization, the open enterprise, and the flexible firm all attempt to define completely rational criteria for organizational change. They endeavor to describe standardized second-order procedures and programs for every single case. The processes and programs of these organizational models no longer prescribe routine behavior in the organization, but describe how new problems can be solved. Employees are not told which solution to use when responding to problems; they are told which basic procedures to apply to the solution.

The distinguishing features of type A, type B, or type C organizations are ultimately unimportant. Companies do not derive stability

---

17 See, e.g., (Toffler 1980); see also (Robbins/Finley 1996, 11) and (Starkey 1998, 533).

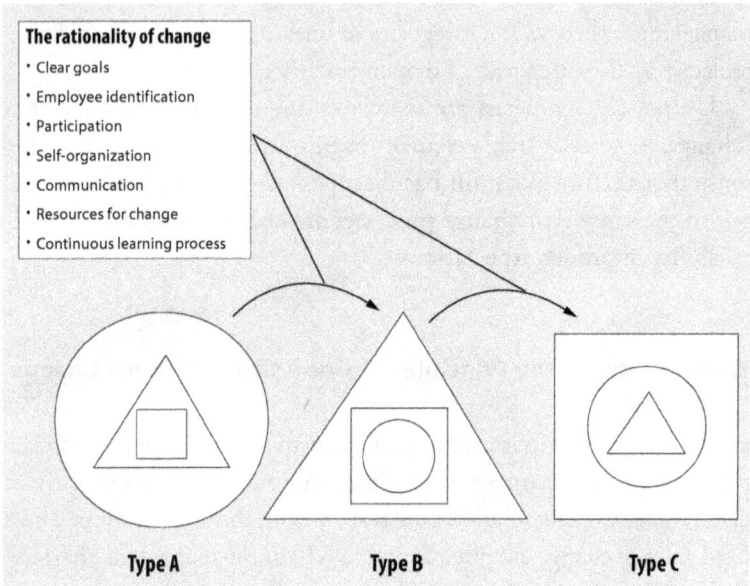

Fig. 6: New Constructs of Rationality: Rationality Derived from the Rule-Based Nature of Organizational Change

and certainty from the assumption that they have found an optimal organizational form. They rely on the fact that with the rules of rational organizational change, they gain enough certainty to continue to exist even under changed environmental conditions.

What exactly are these standardized second-order procedures and programs based on? What are the rules of rational organizational change?

There is of course no final authority to define the basic principles of good organizational change. However, it is easy to see that the charters, basic principles, and disciplines of organizational change have a great deal in common. Regardless of whether the principles invoke learning, intelligence, knowledge, progress, openness, or flexibility, they are similar in many areas. This is because organizations do not develop rules behind closed doors, but base them on approaches that have proven successful in other organizations. Specialized literature, training courses, new hires, consulting firms, conferences, regular get-togethers

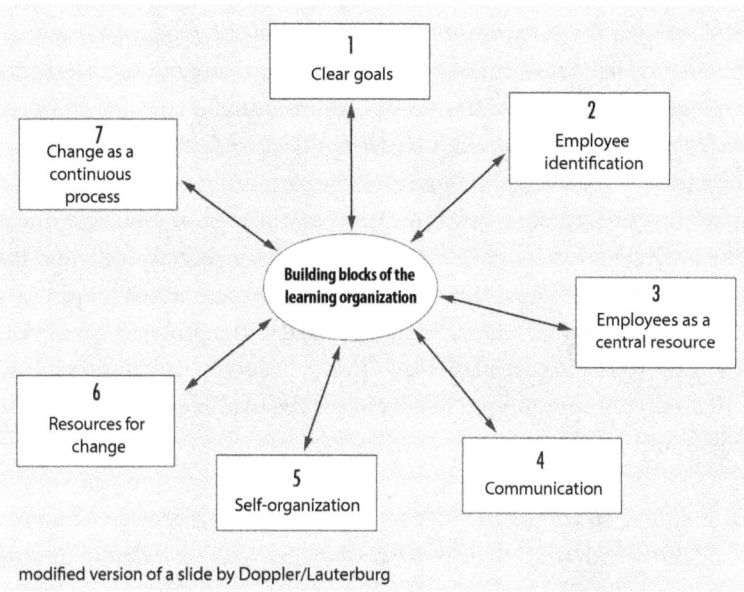

Fig. 7: The Principles of the Learning Organization—Rules for Change Management

for entrepreneurs, and other exchanges contribute to the similarity of the criteria for good organizational change.

The many change management books, organizational models, and consultancy presentation slides can be condensed into seven basic principles. At first glance, these principles may seem quite plausible—and they may even provide organizations with a degree of stability in their change processes. As the next chapter shows, though, the only reason they appear rational is that their problematic aspects are suppressed.[18]

---

[18] I have distilled these seven principles from a large number of English and German books, from articles in the trade press and essay collections, and from presentation slides prepared by consultants. In my opinion, they are supported by every organization, at least verbally. Furthermore, we can derive the ideal-typical learning organization from them. However, because some of the principles may contradict each other in terms of their general focus (e.g., clear goals versus resources for change), the rationality construct underlying them is in fact quite fragile. I am willing to accept the incompleteness of my list because most of the other principles of organizational change also support my argument.

1. Clear goals—The first fundamental principle of good organizational change is that organizations must precisely define the objective of a change project and break it down into meaningful steps. The change manager's credo is that for a change project to deliver useful results, it must be undertaken in a goal-oriented fashion. On the basis of a careful, systematic analysis of the problem, the organization determines the project's concrete objectives and criteria for success. It divides the project into individual steps and chooses the method for monitoring progress. As part of this systematic approach, the problem is analyzed in order to decide on a solution. This solution is broken down into concrete concepts and implemented. In the final phase of the project, the results are reviewed.

2. Employee identification—The second principle is that employees need to identify with the change process. Organizations should not motivate employees by means of money and pressure alone. They must ensure that employees recognize and acknowledge the usefulness of the work processes and decisions.

3. Focus on people—The third principle is that employees must be involved. Organizations must increasingly shift the focus to people with all their individuality. The objective is to align the employees' interests, needs, and experiences with the change process and to open up the organization to new perspectives.

4. More communication—The fourth principle emphasizes communication on change. Management must try to persuade employees and make them understand the necessity of unpopular measures. It is crucial not only that information flow from top to bottom, but also that the organization engage in an active communication process. This is why a special communication concept should be developed for larger, more comprehensive projects.

5. Greater self-organization—The fifth principle is self-organization. Employees should not be told how to respond to environmental changes, but should be allowed to respond to challenges in an autonomous fashion. The goal is to avoid time-consuming, nerve-racking coordination processes between top and bottom. Problems should be addressed and innovative solutions should be developed in the units where these problems crop up.

6. Sufficient resources for change—The sixth principle is that there should be adequate scope for innovation within the organization. Human and material resources and reserves should be made available so that the organization can experiment with them.

7. Continuous learning—The seventh principle is that change should not be a one-time affair, but should be organized as a continuous learning process. The aim of this process is to improve the organization's adaptability and capacity for innovation.

These rules of organizational change are not new. Many of the principles were articulated when organizational development first emerged as a humanistic consulting approach (see, e.g., Lewin 1951) and it was assumed that the close integration of employees into the organization reflected the goals of human-friendly design. However, because the arguments of organizational developers were heavily focused on the question of human design, they were not fully compatible with organizational logic, which is geared to efficiency and effectiveness.

Because of the perceived turbulence in the outside world, the employee-focused principles of change management are currently regarded as the key factors of economic success. These principles are fleshed out in everyday operations in companies, administrations, and organizations. For example, agreements are reached on how change processes are to be implemented in organizations. Participation rights are established and appeal mechanisms are created. Management might promise, for instance, that within the scope of the change processes workers will not be laid off.

3.2. Signs of the Rationality of Change

What we are seeing here is of course not a simple shift from the "rationality of organizational structures" to the "rationality of change processes." Different conceptions of order overlap in business practice. The new, change-oriented models do not (yet?) predominate. In most organizations, these two ideas exist side by side.

However, there is a clear trend toward developing rules for organizational change. The new understanding of rationality is already leaving its mark on many spheres. The fields in which managers work, the tools they use, as well as the description of tasks by consultants, are increasingly based on a new understanding of rationality. The stabilization of rational organizational structures has receded into the background. The skilled, well-planned implementation of change processes is what counts. In what follows, I will describe four trends in very rough strokes:

Organizational Leadership—from Manager to Leader

In the past, it sufficed for the leaders of an organization to inform shareholders, financial institutions, public authorities, political leaders, customers, and employees that they had the right strategy for the current situation. All these leaders needed to do was to announce that they had the proper internationalization, diversification, merger, outsourcing, or rationalization strategy to meet current demands.

Nowadays this impression alone no longer suffices to establish the legitimacy of top managers. If this was all they communicated, they would leave themselves open to the charge that the respective strategies are suitable only for the current situation, but do not prepare the organization for possible future changes in its environment. They would confront the criticism that the organization is "over-managed" and lacks the capacity to cope with a turbulent environment.

This is one of the reasons that management literature has been repeatedly demanding a shift from "manager" to "leader." Managers are stuck in the present, while leaders give more thought to the future. Managers merely introduce effective organizational structures and manage these structures in a bureaucratic fashion, while leaders offer visions, create enthusiasm for new ideas, and give employees the necessary scope for change. One of the key characteristics of a leader is that she sees herself as an agent of change, learns throughout her life, and can handle complexity and uncertainty.

In an environment that emphasizes the rationality of change, top managers are increasingly being forced to convey the impression that they have suitable formulas for organizational change. They must prove not only that they have the usual value-creating activities under control, but that they have command of the new discipline of business change.

Middle Management—from a Buffering Unit to Support for Change Processes

Middle management is probably the domain where we can best see the transformation of rationality in organizations. With its protective function, middle management used to be responsible for keeping environmental uncertainty away from the workers in the productive core. Middle managers translated conflicting environmental requirements into detailed instructions and monitored their compliance. Through the selective use of "uncertainty processing skills," they ensured organizational stability. As noted above, these duties are becoming ever more superfluous in a large number of organizations: uncertainties, complexities, and contradictory data are now being communicated directly to the employees in the productive core, who adapt their organizational structures to environmental changes in an autonomous fashion.

An initial response to these changes was to declare middle management unnecessary. The very people who had carried out company restructurings in the past now became its victims. The traditional responsibilities, employment opportunities, and career chances of middle managers were seen as eroding. Henceforward the primary task of middle management—the handling of uncertainty—would be performed by workers in production.

The middle managers who faced streamlining pressures were reassured with promises of important new roles, such as employee consultation, coaching, personnel development, the management and coordination of reorganization projects, support for the relaunch of manufacturing processes, mediation in conflict situations, and the initiation and support of change initiatives (for a critical discussion, see Sturdy/Wright/Wylie 2014).

These tasks reveal a fundamental shift. Middle management is increasingly responsible for ensuring stability in comprehensive change processes. Once specialists for rational production, they are now specialists for rational change.

New Management Techniques

Many management techniques of the past were billed as formulas for a supposedly optimal organizational form. In structure-oriented management models, instruments were developed to implement optimal organizational structures. Associations concerned with rationalizing economic processes developed standard procedures for successful organizational design. Essay collections summarized proposals for rational procedural guidelines and described optimal product and production methods.

However, these management techniques are suffering from ever shorter half-lives. The leading standardization and rationalization associations are in a state of crisis. They can hardly keep up with the development of instruments for the launch of optimal organizational structures.

As can be observed, most of the recent management tools focus on providing methods for redesigning, reorganizing, and realigning businesses. The list of promising new management tools—benchmarking, balanced scorecards, the ISO 9000 quality family, etc.—seems endless. Through the use of popular terms such as "knowledge management" and "change management," an attempt has been made to systematically structure these new management tools and to market them as a complete package. A specific feature of these concepts is that they are no longer billed as supporting *one* new optimal organizational form but as being neutral in relation to the organizational structure. A few examples:

Benchmarking: Benchmarking involves searching for and finding the supposedly best organizational practices. This method of competitor analysis does not focus on the many lesser formulas for success that are adopted by highly successful organizations. Rather, its unique feature is that it takes a systematic approach to copying other organizations' ideas—in other words, it creates its own system in the search for best practices or role models.

Balanced scorecard: Under this method, managers use key figures to evaluate their performance from a variety of perspectives. Different factors are questioned and analyzed, including financial situation, customer and employee orientation, quality assurance, process focus, and learning and growth prospects. The various measurement instruments represent a kind of management cockpit in which all the relevant organizational processes are displayed. Proponents promise that the cockpit will help managers not only fly their standard "routes" (meaning the "one best way") but also venture into entirely unknown territory.

ISO 9000 family: The objective of these quality standards is not to establish a predefined organizational form. The standards merely serve to ensure the reproducibility of organizational processes. Even if it is often criticized, the goal of ISO quality standards is not the certification of product quality, but the certification of the quality assurance system. They provide standards for documenting quality-relevant processes.

In the case of all these management techniques, what counts most are not the results of one-time use, but the fact that the confident mastery of tools enables the organization to survive even in turbulent environments.

The Changing Conception of Consulting

In the consulting sector, too, we are seeing a new focus on processes. Even the larger consulting firms that once limited themselves to submitting reports to management teams are now supporting change processes. Within the framework of process consulting, organizations are engaging in reflection and change. Consultants are increasingly seeing it as their job to help clients gain new perspectives by challenging them and offering them new ideas.

Consultants do not promise clients an expert's certainty in keeping with organizational goals. Rather, they provide the guarantee that they will skillfully design a change process whose results are largely open. They show that they possess certainty in dealing with uncertainty. Long reference lists, frequent mentions in the business press, and longstanding client relationships help them convey the proper impression.

In all of this consultants also work with rules, but these rules are based not on organizational structure, but on the way change is supposed to take place.

The Planning-Related Duplication of the Change Process—Ideas about Planned Change

From the ideas about rationality that are oriented to organizational change, people normally draw a conclusion that has far-reaching consequences. Change process can be planned, controlled, and managed by organization designers if the charters, basic principles, and disciplines of organizational change are taken sufficiently into account and if the proven change management tools are used. The underlying assumption is that the objectives of a change project can be achieved if it is based on the models of good organizational change.

Where do these ideas about predictable and manageable change come from?

The rules for good organizational change result in a planning-related duplication of the change process. The phenomenon of duplication is known from attempts to scientifically plan production processes in the value-added core. Here the proponents of optimal organizational structures attempted to create a precise, binding plan for work processes and to specify every step on the basis of this plan. As a result, the work process existed twice: once as a blueprint for optimal production flow, and once as the real activities of employees. Management attempted to align the real working process as closely as possible with the optimal flow.

This type of planning-related duplication also occurs in companies that use the management models geared toward organizational change. The proponents of change concepts assume that by using the rules for good organizational change, they can plan change processes in great detail and then effectively put them into action. On the basis of change management rules, they create a plan for the optimal course of change. Similar to the work process, the change process now exists in duplicate: once as a plan for change, and once as a real change process within the organization.

In most change projects, the consequences of this planning-related duplication are easy to see. A team develops a master plan for a company reorganization based on an analysis of the problem. This master plan consists of a catalogue of solutions, a flow chart for the change project, and predefined milestones. When developing the master plan, the team often works together with consultants, who provide ideas and share experiences from other consulting projects. A blueprint emerges that shows how organizational change is to be implemented. A complex project architecture is created to implement the master plan. In a steering committee, members of senior management make basic decisions and specify rough guidelines, supported by employee representatives. On the level below the steering committee, in so-called program and support committees, program managers break down the basic specifications into concrete actions and discuss actual problems in the change project. On the next lower level, the employees who are both directly and indirectly affected implement the guidelines in working groups.

This project hierarchy is supported by many staff positions within the change project. A "sponsor" who holds a position at the tip of the hierarchy strengthens the various initiatives through her authority. The sponsor is responsible for making resources available to others, facilitating access to top management, providing advice, and, if necessary, supporting the group as a coach. Marketing committees are set up to promote the change process internally. As an organized group of "change evangelists," these marketers present the new ideas in an enthusiastic, committed fashion. Their goal is to encourage and reinforce a willingness to change. In addition, consultants, coaches, and researchers work on the various project levels assisting the groups with the change processes.

Various techniques are used to support this form of change management. Employee surveys and interviews are conducted, process models are developed, and "sensor teams" are assembled to keep their finger on the pulse of the organization. An entire range of change techniques are now available. In extreme cases, workshops with appealing names such as "Genesis" or "Turbo" are held to get the organization quickly into shape.

The goal of these extensively planned change projects is to align the real-world change project with the carefully elaborated master plan. The plan can be changed in minor ways in the course of the project, but the primary focus is to create enthusiasm for the project among employees. As part of the planning-related duplication of the work process in the past, the task of management was to smoothly integrate machines and employees into the planned value-creation process; in the planning-related duplication of a change process, by contrast, the task of the (change) manager is to extensively integrate employees into the planned change project.

The planning-related duplication of change processes shows quite clearly how approaches from the world of machines have been transferred to the field of organizational change. In process-oriented management, plans must be reconciled with reality, as is the case with the operation of machines. As one change management textbook puts it, during the "production" of change, companies must constantly monitor and regulate the continuity of the processes, much like line production in the chemicals industry. At all the critical junctures, sensors must determine "temperatures" and "mixing ratios." In response to the slightest deviations from target values, management must make finely calibrated adjustments to the process.

3.3. From Rational Organizational Architectures to the Principles of Rational Change

In summary, we can say that the new management concepts such as the learning organization, the knowledge-based company, and the evolutionary enterprise have brought about a fundamental shift in the way models are designed. Organizations face the dilemma of having to focus on stability and change at the same time. The manner in which the models of good organizational change attempt to resolve this dilemma is the exact opposite of the method used by traditional models. In the new concepts, the relationship between uncertainty and certainty, between change and stability, is reversed.

This shift can be traced in four steps.

Beyond Hyperstability and Hyperflexibility

The traditional bureaucratic model was based on the assumption of a hyperstable organizational form. Certainty and controllability were its main principles.

Mechanisms for handling uncertainty were then selectively incorporated into the dominant stability-oriented system. In the models of Taylorism, lean management, and business process reengineering, change-oriented units such as human resources, quality control, and purchasing sought to ensure that the work in the stability-oriented core could be carried out according to rational criteria. The various stability-oriented models differ in terms of the exact role they assign to the change-oriented units.

Because the environment is supposedly changing at an increasingly rapid pace, there is now less faith in the idea of a single organizational structure that is optimally attuned to all environmental conditions. The perceived turbulence has made it nearly impossible to present formal organizational structures as instrumental-rational. A growing number of organizations have ceased searching for the ideal method to achieve organizational success—at least officially. "Prefabricated" organizational

Model No. 1: The Hyperstable Organization with No Mechanism for Coping with Uncertainty		
Model: hyperstable organization with no mechanism for coping with uncertainty	Solution to stability/change dilemma	Central problems
• Bureaucratic ideal-type	• One-sided emphasis on stability • Disregard of change requirements	• Incapable of adapting to environmental changes

Table 1: Model No. 1: The Hyperstable Organization with No Mechanism for Handling Uncertainty

Model No. 2: The Stable Organization with a Limited Integrated Ability to Cope with Uncertainty		
Model: stable organization with a limited integrated ability to cope with uncertainty	Solution to the stability/change dilemma	Central problems
• Taylorism • Lean management • Business process re-engineering	• Stability-oriented rational core • Change-oriented units to translate environmental fluctuations into clear instructions for the productive, value-creating core	• Lengthy adaptation processes • Problems creating motivation for change processes • Limited ability to register environmental change

Table 2: Model No. 2: Stable Organization with a Limited Integrated Ability to Process Uncertainty

Model No. 3: The Hyperflexible Organization with No Focus on Stability		
Model: The hyperflexible organization with no focus on stability	Solution to stability/change dilemma	Central problems
• Adhocracies • Holacracies • Teal Organization • Chronically unfrozen systems	• One-sided emphasis on change • Disregard of stability requirements	• High level of uncertainty in the value-creation process • Tendency to disintegrate • Danger of self-dissolution

Table 3: Model no. 3: The Hyperflexible Organization with No Focus on Stability

Model: The change-oriented organization with integrated stabilization mechanisms	Solution for the stability/ change dilemma	Central problems
• Learning organization • Agile Systems • Knowledge-based company • Evolutionary enterprise	• Orientation toward change • Stability derived from reliable rules of change management	• The blind spots of the good rules of change management (discussed in the next chapter)

Table 4: Model No. 4: The Change-Oriented Organization with Integrated Stabilization Mechanisms

models such as lean management and business reengineering have lost their luster. The long idealized view of Japan and the United States—where many of these organizational concepts first emerged—has given way to increasingly critical assessments.

According to the "quantum theory" of organizational change, after a long phase of optimal, relatively stable organizational structures, the next stable structure is established in a kind of revolution. Currently, though, a growing number of observers have expressed skepticism that under the conditions prevalent in the twenty-first century this theory is still valid. Economists Paul Evans and Yves Doz (Evans/Doz 1992, 95), for instance, have called for organizational concepts that are so dynamic that they can facilitate permanent revolutionary developmental processes in organizations. This demand is fulfilled by the management concepts oriented toward transformation and change. However, it would be too taxing for an organization to have to shift completely into change mode. Chronically unfrozen systems have a tendency to disintegrate and dissolve.

This is why so many discussions in management literature revolve around the question of how stability can be achieved in the organizations that are oriented toward transformation and change. One trick used by organizations is to create bodies of rules not for the rational transaction of everyday business, but for the rational design of learning and change. The organizations hope that with these rules they will at least be able to achieve rationality in the design of change—second-order rationality, as it were. What is crucial here is the attempt to define rational rules that are robust enough to withstand errors by both members of the organization and external parties.

Here the relationship between certainty and uncertainty is reversed. The learning organization, the knowledge-creating company, and the evolutionary enterprise are based on the assumption of precarious organizational structures. These structures are secured by the stable rules of organizational change. The rules of learning and change are seen as providing certainty in uncertainty.

Shifting the Focus of Management, Consulting, and Organizational Research

If this fundamental shift in the management discussion continues—and there is every reason to believe it will—there will be far-reaching consequences for management, consulting, and research. The management of companies, administrations, hospitals, universities, and associations will increasingly evolve into the management of organizational change. The focus of organizational consulting will shift from designing optimized, rational organizational structures for the respective environmental conditions to designing "good" and supposedly rational rules of organizational change. Organizational research will devote more attention to the processes of organizational change than to organizational structures.

The current challenge is to expand the hard-won insights into the design of rational, supposedly optimal organizational structures to include an examination of the rational, good rules of organizational change. In the past, it was only possible to develop rational organizational structures by suppressing all of the contradictions associated with this rationality. It is therefore fair to assume that the only reason the good rules of organizational change now appear to be rational is that various fundamental problems have also been suppressed. The next chapter will provide some initial insight into the blind spots of the various models that are based on these good rules of organizational change. My goal is to show that the blind spots caused by the implementation of the models of the learning organization and the knowledge-based company can have dangerous consequences for organizations.

4.
The Blind Spots of the Learning Organization—Seven Contradictions in the Rules of Good Organizational Change

"There are two sides to everything."
Brigitte Saipp

Almost all of the stories about successful change processes that are told at conferences or in articles contain the idea of the systematic planning, management, and control of organizational change. These stories often center on rationally planned and controlled change. The entrepreneurial "stars" are those managers who succeed in getting their staff excited about an idea and transforming their companies so that they benefit from this idea. They are the (intellectual) sons and daughters of rationalist business leaders such as Henry Ford, who invented the assembly line, and Taiichi Ohno, who created lean production—thinkers who managed to radically transform organizations in a rational planning and control process.

There may be organizations that have managed to systematically plan, manage, and control change in this way. At times the pressure on organizations may be so great, management so powerful, consultants so integrative, and solutions so clear that the rational concept of planned and predictable change may bring success. Particularly in less complex organizations, it may indeed be possible to induce employees to work toward a jointly developed goal with such commitment that a rationally planned and managed change project can be successfully pulled off. At times change processes seem to resemble the programming of trivial machines and change processes seem almost automatically to lead to success.

But a growing number of organization designers, developers, and change managers are moving away from the traditional view of organizational processes in management theory. With respect to the overall organization, they are expressing doubts that processes intrinsic to a system can be precisely managed and controlled. They are distancing themselves from the idea that it is possible to make accurate predictions about developments and are demanding that organizations no longer be regarded as trivial machines.

Against this backdrop, it is all the more paradoxical that most change management methods and approaches continue to be based on controllability, "forecastability," defined procedures, exact planning, and established response patterns. There continues to be a belief that managers can use plans and concepts to determine an organization's future—and that optimally designed change processes can establish viable links between deficiencies, causes, goals, and measures. When creating plans and implementing ideas, managers often employ tools and concepts that seem more suitable for modifying trivial machines than for designing complex systems.

Admittedly, these ideas about predictability in change management are far removed from the simplistic authoritarian ideas about control that served as guiding principles of Taylorist organizations. Now, as part of a holistic approach, it is not only technical, structural, and economic elements that are incorporated into planning, but interpersonal ones as well. Under the heading of holistic thinking and action, attention is paid to written and unwritten rules and laws, to motivation, identification, and the interconnections between the various factors.

Furthermore, the planning concepts of change management have come to include feedback loops, continuous interim analyses, and new definitions. They are based on the idea that the corresponding methodological tools, which are adapted to changes in a measure's planning environment, make it possible to plan and control the processes of change. Practitioners are not abandoning the idea of controllability, but are developing more elaborate forms of control: ever shorter feedback and control loops, ever more sensitive sensors, and ever more flexible control centers. They have distanced themselves from simplistic assumptions of a mechanistic order, only to replace these with a relatively sophisticated cybernetics of static rules and loops. However, this approach is still founded on the idea that behavior in organizations can generally be planned and ultimately can be controlled. While organizations are not machines that are controlled from above, they nonetheless consist of regulated processes.

Common Explanations of the Difficulties of Implementing the Learning Organization

The problems confronted when implementing the learning organization are then explained from the perspective of rationally planned change. A large number of companies, administrations, and organizations claim to be learning organizations, but if they are examined more closely, we find a glaring discrepancy between theory and practice. Many organizations appear to be implementing the rules of good organizational change only to a limited degree. In keeping with the logic of the planning-related duplication of the change process, proponents point out that while the plans are based on the proper principles, there continue to be problems with implementation. It is common in organizational practice and the management literature to underscore the implementation difficulties instead of calling the principles themselves into question. Scientifically based, statistically supported explanations are offered that describe the large number of difficulties, the opposition to the change process, and the many obstacles placed in its way.[19]

At first glance, it may seem plausible to explain the implementation difficulties by pointing to the strong influence exerted on employees by the old hierarchical organization, which was divided into functional areas. From this perspective, employees have a mental block that is undermining the change initiatives. Particularly in

---

19 See, for example, the list in (Hussey 1998, 588ff.) concerning opposition to change. One of the most intelligent lists of possible reasons for the resistance to change can be found in (Eccles/Nohria 1992).

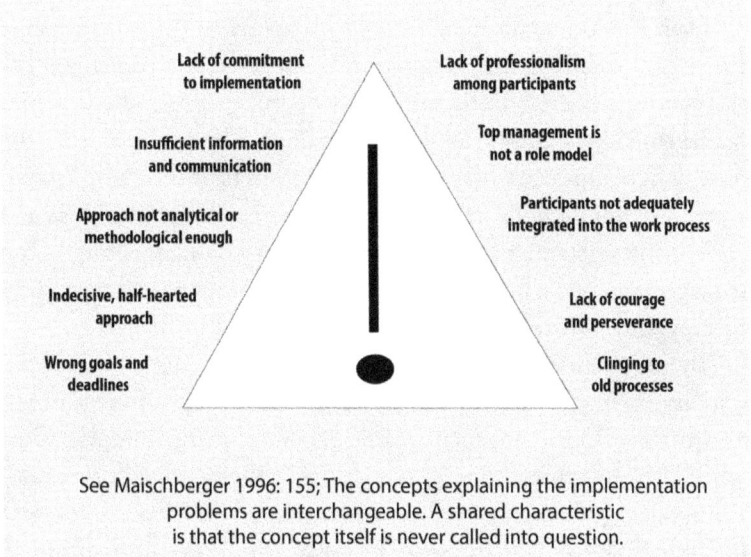

Fig. 8: Typical Explanations of Failed Change Projects

situations where the organization does not yet have its back against the wall, employees do not see the necessity of change—not until it is much too late.

Another common explanation is that the change process has not been sufficiently "marketed" in the organization. Organizational change has not been effectively promoted and employees do not understand what the organization wishes to achieve by it. "Change communication" has been inadequate and no corresponding information policy has been created to get employees on board.

It is even more popular (and particularly lucrative for external consultants) to attribute opposition within the organization to poorly planned change processes. The failure of these processes is blamed on a number of factors, including diffuse objectives, blurry visions, the unfavorable composition of project teams, insufficient support from top management, poor employee integration, and overly ambitious schedules. As a result, the organization lacks suitable tools to successfully implement the change management project.

Even if it is not normally acceptable to say so (perhaps because the person offering this explanation has worked as a consultant for the company), the failure can always be put down to the fact that management has simply not gone far enough. The responsible parties have ended a measure prematurely, or, in terms of its commitment, scope, and duration, the change process itself has been insufficient and contained targets that were not ambitious or visionary enough. Top management, as the provider of impetus, has not supported the radical therapy unconditionally. It simply lacked the will to change.

These explanations are familiar to us from the discussion of the stability-oriented concepts that preceded the concept of the learning organization. Criticisms such as "lack of commitment to implementation," "lack of courage and perseverance," "clinging to old processes," "insufficient information and communication," "inadequate integration of employees into the work process," "no powerful coalition of leaders," "wrong goals and deadlines," "not rooted in organizational culture" and "lack of professionalism among participants" all have been used to explain the failure of lean management and reengineering campaigns.

Simple Solutions

What all these explanatory approaches have in common is that the solutions to the problems are obvious. One can easily distill the six, seven, or eight cardinal errors made in change processes into six, seven, or eight steps for successful change. The solutions are explicitly provided by the explanations—in the tradition of many traditional management approaches.

First of all, seminars and training courses can be held to prevent employees from clinging to old patterns of thought and behavior. These seminars provide employees with information before, during, and after change initiatives and teach them techniques for effective communication, brainstorming, and conflict resolution. Motivational training and the techniques of group dynamics can help employees overcome their fear of change. In extreme cases, they (or the managers themselves) can be sent on "power days," where they are forced to walk on hot coals in the hope that this exercise will give them the courage to tackle change.

Second, one of the best strategies to combat the fear of change is "inform, inform, inform." Based on the example of management, which is supposed to "live" the new culture, employees can be made to feel enthusiastic about the new philosophy. As part of this solution, champions or evangelists of change provide information about its benefits and create excitement about the envisioned measures. In addition, a special marketing policy can be developed for the change process. This can entail pinning notices on the organization's bulletin board, publishing appealing articles in its newsletter, and producing videos, all in the attempt to instill the new mentality in employees and persuade them to identify with the new culture. The major role played in change projects by the PR departments of companies such as ABB and Volvo demonstrate that the marketing of change has now become a central element of change initiatives. The same is shown by the growing number of advertising agencies that are active in the field of organizational consulting.

Third, there is a large variety of materials and experts available to protect organizations from the pitfalls of change management. Books about change management now fill entire bookshelves. Change workshops and change management seminars are enjoying great success. A growing number of human resource consultants are specializing in organizational process support. The first "change controllers" and "chief change officers" have entered the marketplace and are systematically planning change and supporting its implementation. On the list of the most popular manager types, change managers have replaced increasingly obsolete rivals. Instead of "status quo" managers who play only defense and work according to the old rules, companies want open, go-getting change managers who are able to recognize and seize the opportunities for innovative action.

Fourth, a lack of single-mindedness in the change process can be remedied by greater decisiveness. It may sound surprisingly simple, but one way to overcome a lack of determination is through more determined action. Quite a few managers take the easy way out by attributing the failure of their recommended measures to indecisiveness on the part of the workforce. A courageously communicated "keep on keeping on" can encourage managers and employees alike to move forward in a decisive manner.

All of these approaches to solving the problems linked to change processes are based on a very simple organizational concept: growth. In other words, more training, more information, more motivation, more advice, and more exchange. Using these approaches, managers typically respond to requirements and their associated problems by creating new internal positions for organizational and personnel development, bringing in more consultants, and devoting more time to change.

Dispensing with Problems by Personalizing Errors

What these approaches also have in common is that they start with human beings—an approach that at first glance may seem well founded. They seek to explain the depressing discrepancy between the ambitious plans for change and the sobering reality of change processes by pointing to omissions on the part of human capital. According to this logic, the greatest risk faced by successful organizations that are undergoing change is human beings. True to the tradition of industrial psychology, problems are personalized and explained psychologically. The difficulties in change processes are attributed to a variety of factors: the influence exerted by old structures, inadequate communication on the necessity of change, a lack of determination to implement change, and insufficient expertise on the "how" of implementation. The argument is that, due to the imperfect state of human beings, change processes ultimately cannot be implemented as originally planned.

A special feature of the organization is that virtually all events can be attributed to individuals. This is why concepts are often offered that promise improvement if management *only* reach decisions more quickly, if group spokespersons *only* focus more heavily on quality, if executives *only* think more entrepreneurially, or if sales staff *only* forwards orders more quickly to production. The organization can expect improvement if people cooperate more closely, work harder to achieve specific goals, and embrace these goals more passionately.

In many situations, it can certainly make sense to personalize problems—and the solutions as well. To a certain extent, it can be useful for collective action to assign failures, like successes, to individuals. Because people are a tangible aspect of organizations, it is easy to make them responsible for mistakes. One particular individual bears responsibility for a problem and thus relieves the pressure on the organization to search for other sources of errors, which often blocks action (Brunsson 1989, 202–3).

This alleviating function can frequently be observed at the managerial level. At first glance, it may not be clear why top executives who have made grave errors should be given high severance packages when they are fired. However, if we consider the fact that within the system, errors need to be linked to individuals, the process is quite understandable. The severance pay is often just a form of forced remuneration that is awarded to an employee for accepting responsibility for an error. If a car company is accused of industrial espionage, it may be effective for the company to blame a high-level executive and dismiss this executive as a way of clearing itself of the espionage charge.

A similar function is fulfilled by organizational consulting firms. Although it is easily overlooked, consultants bring a key advantage to organizations, above and beyond their expertise. Consultants make it easy to personalize—and thus to dispense with—the problems encountered in risky, complex change processes. Companies assign most of the responsibility for a change process to a consultant and are thus in a position to free themselves relatively quickly from the associated problems. The disposable nature of many consulting concepts and the ease with which consultants can be fired both enable companies to sacrifice the concepts and the consultants should the necessity arise. In the final analysis, the consultants' fee, which in some cases can be quite high, contains a bonus for taking responsibility for the problems in change processes and for serving as the fall guy in crises.

Despite these plausible reasons for seeking the causes of problems in individual behavior, we must not forget that such explanations are based on a limited view: they continue to be shaped by traditional management theory. Under this theory, organizations are able to function according to their own blueprints (operating plans, organizational charts, schedules of responsibility, etc.) only if individuals subordinate themselves to the organization's formal structures. Organizational processes can run smoothly only if employees follow the rules and regulations of these formal structures.

In other words, human beings are portrayed as the wrenches in the gears of what is basically an effective, well-oiled piece of machinery. From this angle, the concealment of errors, the presentation of false facts, favoritism, nepotism, intrigue, and the manipulation and withholding of information are not the effects of the system or of organizationally sensible strategies, but aberrations and perversions of rational plans. The verbosity, ineptitude, hypocrisy, bad moods, and instability associated with organizational life are portrayed as the pathologies of an organization that operates rationally as a whole. They are not regarded as functional and efficient for the organization.

The solutions are ultimately based on the hope that organizations can "de-problematize" the human factor through training, effective organization, and the optimal design of organizational change. The thinking runs like this: if only we work hard enough on human nature, if only we convey the need for change adequately enough, if only we work on perfecting our routines and change processes, we will be able to master these processes without any difficulty.

The Difficulty of Change Processes—
the Seven Contradictions of Organizational Change

These explanations of the problems that are associated with the learning organization have one special feature: by constantly pointing to the technical mistakes in implementation, they make all criticism of the promoted principles taboo. They suggest that the approach can be

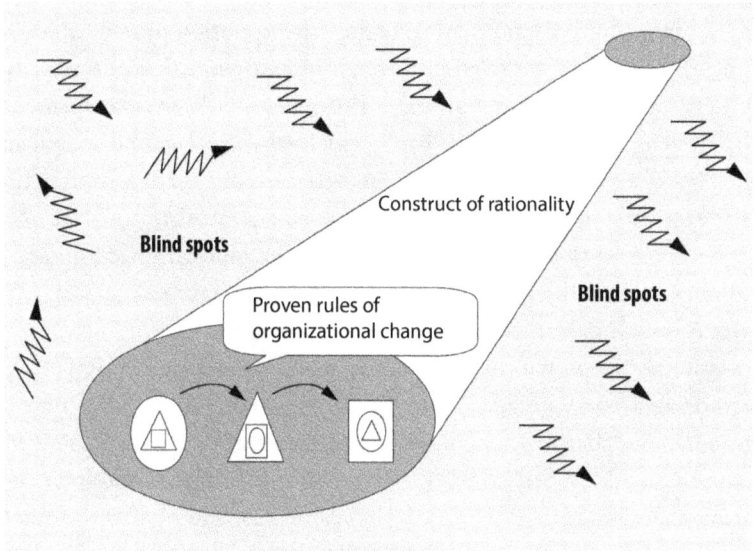

Fig. 9: The Learning Organization's Blind Spots

successful if professional standards are adhered to in the implementation phase. Given the positive connotation of terms such as objectives, identification, communication, participation, and self-organization, it might not enter anyone's mind that the principles of the learning organization themselves could be faulty.

It is precisely this largely taboo perspective that I would like to expand upon in this section. My thesis is that the difficulties and pathologies in organizations that are undergoing change are not attributable to the employees' specific characteristics, faults, or weaknesses. Rather, they are related to the fundamental problems of organizational change—problems that are based on a large number of contradictions, conflicting goals, and dilemmas.

It is only possible to portray the learning organization as a promising management strategy by systematically suppressing the contradictions, conflicting goals, and dilemmas associated with it. This is achieved by describing certain rules of organizational change as good (e.g., clear objectives, employee identification, self-organization, learning) and denouncing and discriminating against the opposing principles (e.g., unclear objectives, motivation through money alone, organization by others, the avoidance of learning). This mentality keeps management from recognizing that these "bad" principles can in fact be beneficial for "good" organizational change. In extreme cases, managers often do not even recognize that these opposing principles exist.

In contrast to this limited perspective, the following sections seek to illustrate the dilemmas associated with organizational change. My aim is to highlight the suppressed elements and reconceptualize organizational change as a contradictory process. Nobel laureate Herbert A. Simon (Simon 1946, 53; Simon 1957, 20) was one of the first scholars to point out that many popular management principles have a lot in common with proverbs. For every proverb and pearl of wisdom it contains, there is a plausible proverb that can be used to express the exact opposite idea. For example, "Opposites attract" is no less persuasive than "Birds of a feather flock together." Likewise, for every piece of advice from a management consultant, there is a piece from another consultant (and sometimes even from the same one) that conveys the exact opposite (Pfeffer/Sutton 2006). For example, one basic principle in business management is that the span of control in organizations should be as small as possible; according to another one, organizations should favor flat hierarchies. Both principles sound plausible, but upon further reflection it is clear that they are incompatible.

Herbert A. Simon had organizational structure in mind when he made these observations about managerial proverbs, but they are also relevant to change processes. If we take a closer look at some of the proven insights from organizational research, we see that for almost all of the postulated principles of organizational change, opposite principles exist that are supported by equally plausible arguments. In the following, I would like to demonstrate that the seven criteria of "good" change management—clear objectives, employee identification, a focus on people, greater communication, greater self-organization, ample resources for change, and continuous learning—are highly problematic. A large number of blind spots are suppressed in portrayals of the learning organization.

In the first part of each section, I will show which arguments are made for the principles of the learning organization. The proverbs of good organizational change often draw their persuasive power from their ability to focus the organization relatively quickly on change. However, when these principles are used, they produce unwanted side effects that threaten to restrict the organization's adaptability over the medium and long term. This problem will be addressed in the second part of each section. The definition of objectives prevents flexibility in the change process (4.1). If employees identify with products, organizational units, or processes too strongly, change in these areas will be especially difficult (4.2). If employees are closely integrated into change processes, many different interests need to be considered. It can be difficult to create a coherent whole (4.3). Communication is necessary, but it can easily lead to communication overload (4.4). Self-organization can be useful, but patterns are often adopted that staff know from outside their organization (4.5). Creating scope for change can also make sense, but may cause the organization to overlook streamlining potential (4.6). A successful learning process may establish structures that are later difficult to break up (4.7). In the third part of each section, I will show that there are good reasons to promote the seven "counter-proverbs" of the learning organization: unclear goals and visions, motivation through money alone, people as a means to an end, external organization, the reduction of buffers, learning avoidance, and the prevention and disruption of communication through hierarchies. These principles may at first seem unusual, but they do more to ensure that the organization is open to change than many of the learning organization's "good" principles (4.8).

4.1. The Dilemma of Objectives—Precisely Defined Goals Provide Guidance, but Reduce Adaptability

There is a widespread belief that an effective vision and a precisely defined objective are required to initiate every change process: scenarios and ideas about effective organizations are developed and then distilled into these objectives. Precise definitions are intended to ensure that employees are aligned with a joint goal, and precisely formulated objectives enable employees to develop clear decision-making criteria.

The reason that ideas about objectives play such a prominent role in discussions of organizational change is that all the activities in an organization appear to be in the service of such collective goals. The assumption is that anything that does not serve these interests will be modified, changed, or discarded.

After the objectives of the change measures are defined and the relevant organizational model is established, organizations go to great lengths to publicize the objectives and models internally and to create a true "ideology of change." Comprehensive change concepts and models are published on glossy paper with appealing illustrations. The objectives of change are cast in verse or reduced to catchy acronyms such as TOP plus, WIN, and SUPER. Organizations invite employees to large conferences in sports arenas in order to create a sense of "we" for the change project. A powerful ideology of change is introduced to help overcome the opposition within the organization and the associated problems.

At the same time, organizations need to define the visions, goals, and guidelines of change in such precise terms that their achievability is recognizable. If the objectives and models consist of platitudes, it is difficult to win over employees. As former Unilever CEO Floris Maljers once said dryly, "Being great at everything is not an actionable message." Organizations might be able to handle a certain amount of managerial prose along the lines of "We want to manufacture world-class products for the world market," but if the promoted objectives and ideology of change are limited to such generalities, the effects of the painstakingly developed goals will fizzle out in the lobbies and corridors of organizational headquarters.

In a nutshell: the visions, models, and ideologies of change have the greatest impact when precise goals are articulated, structural changes are defined, realistic numbers are communicated, and clear principles are used. If the goals and the ideology clearly establish what is to be achieved in the change process, employees are more likely to understand the proposed path. The more precise the conception of change, the more precise will be the ideas within the organization as to what is to be achieved by it.

The Advantages of Precisely Defined Goals

Precisely defined objectives and ideologies of change provide answers to the questions posed by employees regarding what needs to happen, why it needs to happen, and how it needs to happen. They make it less necessary to reach fundamentally new decisions before each action. In addition, they temporarily solve the decision-making problems that organizations constantly face because of incompatible alternatives. The objectives of change are ultimately the crystallized manifestations of decisions already taken, and together with the ideology of change, they structure the further decision-making processes.

In extreme cases (which of course only exist in theory), objectives and ideologies can even render decisions unnecessary. They are so precise, so exact, and so narrowly defined that employees are able to translate them into clear actions. The advantage is that the operational framework is clearly laid out for the workforce and thus creates clarity on the path forward. This simplifies coordination between the various participants. Activities in the organization are "orchestrated" in the sense that the argument is simplified. In other words, clearly defined objectives and the belief in a strong organizational ideology have an integrative effect and motivate people to act, because they allow clarity to emerge.

Objectives as Obstacles to Innovation

So far, so good. But objectives, ideals, and ideologies bring a fundamental problem: they limit the scope for change. Employees can be motivated and inspired to do everything that is in line with the narrowly articulated ideology. Precisely defined objectives reduce the variety of actions they can take. In other words, they place limits on creativity. One might even go so far as to claim that precisely defined objectives and ideologies of organizational change make people more narrow-minded, dumber, and discourage rather than encourage innovation.

Only those employees who act within the given framework can assume that they will reach a consensus and gain approval. In certain situations, the framework established by the precisely defined objectives, models, and narrowly defined ideology may be sufficient to effect change. If it is clear from the start that a decision can be made within the given framework, it can make sense for organizations to strengthen such objectives and guiding principles to every extent possible. However, if we can trust the anecdotal evidence from management, organizations are increasingly facing the challenge of having to respond to changing environmental conditions by making rapid, radical changes. A narrowly defined objective places such great limits on their ability to do so that many viable solutions are not even considered. A detailed, elaborately planned strategy impedes adaptation to short-term environmental changes.

Seen from this perspective, precise objectives have a problematic side: they make it difficult to implement changes that no longer suit the organization's original goals. Whereas objectives have a positive effect by orchestrating individual actions in stabile environments, this advantage becomes problematic if the environment changes frequently. If the defined goal needs to be reformed, all the previous specifications prevent the organization from changing course. The rigidity of the objectives proves to be an obstacle.

If management creates a comprehensive list of objectives at the start of the year and agrees on targets with the workforce, it has an efficient coordination instrument at its disposal—provided the environmental conditions remain the same. Otherwise the list becomes a chiseled-in-stone impediment to necessary flexible adaptations within the organization. Target agreements induce employees to focus on the officially agreed specifications. All other factors recede into the background. Employees are justified in resisting if the objectives change suddenly over the course of a year.

Every company whose name describes its corporate objectives faces this problem. A consultancy that defines itself internally and externally as a business process reengineering firm will regret overemphasizing reengineering in its corporate identity when the reengineering wave ebbs.

The four dots in the former logo of the Beiersdorf chemicals group symbolized its four divisions—Cosmed, Medical, Pharma, and Tesa. If Beiersdorf had sold the Medical division and suddenly begun using just three dots in its logo, it would have had a lot of explaining to do to customers and employees.

The Appeal of Unclear Goals and Strategies

These examples make clear that under certain conditions, organizations can be particularly successful if they do without clear goals and ideologies. In turbulent environments, it can be an effective strategy to dispense with strategic planning altogether. The organization might be able to respond especially well to environmental changes precisely because it lacks a clear model, objective, or strategy. Precisely because it does not have any goals, an organization with a "good nose" might find the best path forward.

In this regard, it could be considered a stroke of luck that despite all the efforts by top management, most organizations never commit themselves entirely to clear objectives, models, ideologies, or purposes. Managers should be overjoyed that the formulation of goals and objectives is the subject of intense debate. Again and again, the resources they actually use to achieve objectives become ends in themselves and dominate the focuses in companies. Again and again, new conflicting goals arise, alternative positions are established, and management models are undermined. Again and again, organizational coalitions form that pursue different objectives and alter existing organizational priorities (Cyert/March 1963).

For a limited campaign, it may be useful for an organization to commit itself to clear goals, models, and ideologies, but over the long term the suppression of elements that may appear useless fundamentally jeopardizes the organization's existence. For this reason, the leaders of an organization should not immediately condemn employees who push back against precisely defined objectives, models, and strong organizational cultures. Before firing these employees, they should at least thank them for expanding the organization's scope of action through their opposition.

Constantly Changing Goals—Not a Solution to the Dilemma

For every conflicting goal and every dilemma, solutions are immediately presented. With this in mind, the continuous adaptation of goals and ideologies would appear to be a good business strategy to respond to emerging problems. In many organizations, the goals of the change process are regularly called into question and, if necessary, redefined in intermediary review workshops.

This is certainly a lucrative new market for internal and external consultants, but it does not provide a solution to the dilemma of precisely defined objectives. Continuously adapting goals and constantly modifying the ideologies of change might sound attractive, but both undermine the basic principle behind goals, models, and ideologies. In other words, they are characterized by the fact that they are stable and do not constantly change. At some point, a goal that is constantly changes no longer deserves to be called a goal because goals presuppose permanence. A model that is constantly changed no longer performs the function of a model because it provides no direction. An ideology that is constantly relativized and readjusted no longer deserves to be called an ideology because ideologies require a minimum degree of continuity.

Against this backdrop, it becomes clear why employees respond with cynicism to constant attempts to redefine an organization's goals or all-too-frequent changes to organizational cultures. Employees see these changes as proof that management is inconsistent and unprincipled. Constantly changing ideologies get employees to poke fun at the "vision of the year," the "culture of the month" or the "goal de jour" because they no longer expect any constancy from any of them.

There is no easy solution to this dilemma for organizations. On the one hand, organizations require narrowly defined goals and ideologies in order to get employees excited about projects and provide them with a sense of direction. On the other, the precise definition of goals and ideologies limits the employees' scope for action. In such cases, employees are not prepared for suddenly changing requirements—which is precisely the impediment that the change-committed organization may originally have wanted to prevent.

4.2. The Identification Dilemma—Identifying with Change Processes Reduces Organizational Elasticity

A growing number of organizations are resorting to other means to motivate employees besides financial incentives, pressure, and clever management techniques. They are encouraging employees to identify more strongly with the organization and its products. It is the "pioneering" companies, in particular, that are emphasizing the fact that money alone provides insufficient motivation. Additional important factors include a good working environment and the employees' identification with processes. Humanistic approaches in the field of organizational development are based on the assumption that it can be useful to familiarize employees with an organization's goals. The employees' tasks and responsibilities are defined so comprehensively that it is easy for employees to support these goals. The many diverse requirements—as well as the opportunities for communication and learning—are structured such that employees are made to identify with the organization. The aim here is to make employees understand that it can be fun to assemble high quality scales or fill bags with pudding mix in a self-organized process.

A growing number of managers seem convinced that when employees identify with markets, products, and processes, it enhances their adaptability and capacity for innovation because they then develop a personal interest in making the products or services as efficient and innovative as possible. With visionary enthusiasm, managers tell the story of the stone mason who, when asked about his work, proudly replied, "*We're* building a cathedral" instead of "I'm dressing stone" or "I'm earning a living."

The attempt to use other means of motivation besides money is not new. Shortly before the outbreak of the Second World War, Chester I. Barnard (Barnard 1938, 149–152)—a management pioneer and vice president of AT&T—discovered that it was not enough to strengthen the employees' bonds to a company through wages, promotion opportunities, and status symbols such as large company cars and plush carpets. It was far more important to influence the employees' needs in such a way that employees aligned their own interests with those of the organization of their own accord.

Barnard wanted to inculcate the motives of the organization into all employees—down to the last office boy—as a way to ensure that they identified with organizational goals. He argued that companies should only hire people with the proper motivation structure and in extreme cases fire unmotivated workers in order to make others afraid of losing their jobs. In his eyes, this measure would create stronger ties between employees and the organization (Barnard 1938, 152).

However, identification as a strategy does not need to make use of Barnard's drastic methods. Modern management techniques rely more on changing the working environment to make employees identify with their work. Employees are given more direct contact with markets so that they can observe the effects of their actions. They are assigned comprehensive tasks that ultimately give them the feeling that they are responsible for an entire product or process. They are granted the autonomy to learn from mistakes and change approaches on their own.

This reorganization of the working environment to motivate employees is supplemented by measures that provide staff with information on the meaning of actions and changes. Companies spend a great deal of money ensuring that employees recognize the significance of products and processes. Company newsletters praise new products, celebrate successes, and present revolutionary new production methods. Under catchy names such as "Firm of the Future," these companies attempt to get the workforce excited about change processes. Company managers present new corporate strategies in videos in the hope that their open-mindedness will have a motivating effect on employees.

What is behind the idea that employees should identify with products, processes, and the organization as a whole?

It is assumed that employees will do a better job if the work process is stabilized by personal interests that are aligned with it. The objective of motivation should be linked to the incentives used to achieve it. Change processes are deemed to function better if employees regard their work as a reflection of their personal interests and an organization does not "buy" employee identification through high salaries, bonuses, fancy company cars with luxurious interiors, or incentive trips with celebrities such as Dennis Rodman or Franz Beckenbauer. The general assumption is that people are more most motivated if they are fascinated by a cause and can identify with an organization's values and standards.

Companies hope that employees will become more heavily involved if they identify with their goals. As a rule, people do not invest their entire identity in the organization, but offer only their labor, which is restricted to a defined purpose. The attempt to create stronger bonds between employees and organizations serves to increase their commitment.

At first glance, this method offers advantages to the employees' supervisors. When employees are motivated solely by money, distrustful managers must constantly monitor their actions. Employees provide their labor for a predefined period, but this does not necessarily mean that they work in the interests of the organization without causing difficulties. Supervisors reap benefits if norms, values, and attitudes complement compensation in the form of both money and advancement because norms, values, and attitudes provide a more stable basis for cooperation than the principle of exchanging labor for money.

The Drawbacks to Identification

However, if employees identify strongly with their organization's products or processes, there can also be disadvantages for the organization. It may sound surprising, but the organization forfeits a great deal of adaptability. According to Niklas Luhmann, if employees identify with products or processes, the organization loses its "elasticity." It is difficult for employees to recognize why they need to accept changes that are not consistent with their ideas about processes and products.

This insight allows us to understand what happens when work processes are stabilized by the employees' personal interests. The reinforcement and stabilization of work processes prevents the processes from being easily changed. It would have been very difficult to tell the medieval stonemason who defined himself by his contribution to "building a cathedral" that he had to work at other building sites in the Middle Ages. He can be compared to a soccer player who strongly identifies as a striker and performs well in this position but not in any others.

If employees draw most of their motivation from marketing a particular product, it is hard to motivate them to sell another product. Employees who are responsible for flexibly processing work packages in a group and strongly identify with this group may have motivation problems if they are suddenly assigned to a different area. A member of the sales department who is proud of a particularly modern billing system may become de-motivated if management eliminates this billing system a short time after its launch.

It is certainly a paradox that in the organizations that do everything to ensure that employees support a product or process, it is precisely this identification with a produce or process that places limits on the organization's capacity to act. When employee motivation is especially strong, change will be especially difficult.

The assembly plant of a German carmaker was particularly hard hit by this problem. The plant was originally conceived as a model factory and was presented as such both internally and externally. Many of its workers were proud to be responsible for a relatively large part of assembly. Money was not the sole factor motivating them to go to work. They liked working on a young team with a high level of autonomy. However, the managers who had encouraged employees to identify with their tasks eventually saw that with this policy they were at an impasse. When market changes forced these managers to reduce the autonomy of the assembly plant, there was a massive decline in workforce motivation. According to observers, not a few of the workers expressed the desire to "blow up" parts of the plant—a sentiment that can be put down to their excessive identification with the originally progressive organization of work. If the managers had prevented employees from identifying too strongly with the company and the plant from the start and had made it clear that the purpose of their work was for them to earn money, the workers might have been less motivated, but change could have been implemented more easily.

Separating the Problem of Motivation from Other Organizational Problems

As this example shows, it can make sense to separate the problem of employee motivation from other organizational problems. As economist John Commons (Commons 1924, 284) once pointed out, workers promise the organization that they will use their time, skills, and energy to perform the tasks they have been assigned. In return for a salary, they offer the organization a kind of blank check by agreeing to follow the organization's instructions. They pledge general obedience to instructions that have not yet been clearly formulated.

Drawing on Commons' work, Niklas Luhmann (Luhmann 1964, 90ff.; Luhmann 1973, 128ff.) showed that it can be advantageous for organizations to separate the problem of employee motivation from other problems associated with communication, authority, and meaning. It can make sense to use cash payments, in-kind benefits, and expensive company cars to create stronger bonds between employees and organizations because this practice eliminates these other problems.

Communication: Organizations might try to ensure that internal communications inform and motivate staff at the same time. This approach makes sense if the organization can be certain that the information contributes to employee motivation. But in what organization is that the case? If the organization needs to inform workers that labor intensity must be doubled, it might have difficulty motivating them at the same time. For this reason it is best to use communication channels only to provide information and to leave employee motivation to filthy lucre.

Authority: In the field of management philosophy, a great deal of importance is attached to the idea that managers should create enthusiasm through personal manner and style. In other words, their authority should be based on charm and expertise. It is relatively easy for managers to establish authority in this way in situations where they can play Mr. Nice Guy, but it is much more difficult when crises occur. It can therefore make sense to use cash payments to motivate employees to accept both the organizational hierarchy and their supervisor's authority.

Decision-making: Many organizations call on employees to identify with the organization's decisions. One problem with this approach is that due to the variety of interests within the organization, it is rare for all employees to be in complete agreement with all the decisions. It can therefore be helpful if the objective of a decision does not need to motivate employees to comply with the decision. It can be more effective to pay employees to conduct themselves in a disinterested fashion as regards the decision's objective. The advantage of this "paid indifference" is that employees will follow decisions even if these decisions do not make much sense to them. It also enables managers to focus on whether the planned measure suits the given situation without having to worry about whether the employees will follow the decision.

In other words, organizations can act more flexibly if the problem of employee motivation is detached from other organizational problems. This separate treatment of motivation allows organizations to adapt more quickly and effectively to change. An organization's top management can adjust to new environmental conditions without having to pay excessive attention to the danger that organizational change will de-motivate the workforce. Employees can cope with significant pressure and change because their motivation is secured by cash payments. The willingness to change is reflected in thoughts such as "Who cares about these changes as long as I get my salary each month?"

The advantage of a clear separation between objectives and motivation becomes evident when we take a closer look at organizations that combine the two. Whereas many companies, administrations, and large associations use salaries and wage payments to ensure that organizational goals are distinct from employee motivation, many smaller associations, political initiatives, and clubs connect their members' motivation to their goals and purposes. People join action groups, initiatives, and athletic clubs, for example, because they consider the activities and objectives of these organizations to be important—not because they are paid for their work. Such organizational forms naturally have extremely low personnel costs, but they can run into significant difficulties if their objectives need to be changed. Peace initiatives disband when medium-range missiles are removed from local bases. Political action committees are dissolved when the candidates they support are elected or defeated.

It is worth noting that the associations and initiatives in which objectives and employee motivation are at least partially separated are the ones that are wielding growing influence these days. Greenpeace, which projects an image of itself as an organization with a high degree of employee identification, has been able to increase its influence at least in part because it has separated its aims from its motivation strategies. Its membership fees and donations are in part used to employ a staff whose commitment, initiative, and adaptability are secured not by the belief that the Greenpeace is so "awesome," but by decent pay.

Identifying with Processes and Organizational Units Is Not the Solution

Some organizations have attempted to solve the problem of motivation by encouraging employees to identify with broader processes instead of with narrower fields of responsibility. They believe that it is best if employees identify with customer satisfaction. The thinking runs something like this: I am happy and satisfied if my customer is satisfied. The customer is king and, as the customer's servant, I am ecstatic when my king graces me with a smile and hands over some of the bills in his wallet.

This approach has been promoted above all by the American management guru Peter Senge (Senge 1990). Senge tells the story of a major U.S. steel company that was forced to shut down several of its plants. Although the company offered to train workers for new jobs, its retraining effort failed and the former employees drifted into unemployment. In Senge's view, this failure was due to the fact that the workers identified too closely with their old jobs and were unable to recognize alternatives. "How could I do anything else?" one asked. "I *am* a lathe operator." Senge describes the phenomenon of "I *am* my position" as an impediment to learning and suggests that employees should be made to identify with more comprehensive business processes instead.

What Senge fails to recognize is that he is only replacing "I am my position" as an impediment to learning and change with the new impediment "I am the process" or "I am my organizational unit." After all, employee identification with a profit center, an innovative process, or a complex product is in principle just as problematic as employee identification with a position. It creates the same type of barriers in the face of change. The problem is not that employees identify with a narrowly defined position, but that they identify with something at all.

A bank ran into this problem when it set itself the task of strengthening the bonds between employees and the organization. Employees were given greater autonomy in the execution of their tasks so that they would identify more strongly with work processes. Management hoped that this strategy would make the bank better prepared for the requirements of change in turbulent times. However, the bank then merged with a former competitor, catching many employees off guard, and all of a sudden many of the processes they had organized themselves were eliminated. The previous efforts by management to generate enthusiasm for these processes now took their toll. When asking employees to identify with their processes, the bank had lost organizational elasticity. After the merger, it proved particularly difficult to intervene in areas where identification was the greatest, and these interventions were carried out only at the expense of a massive demotivation of staff.

From this perspective we can see how advantageous it can be to motivate employees using such "vulgar" things as money, cars, and incentives. Money is disconnected from objectives and can be used as a motivator in flexible and practical ways. Nevertheless, money is sometimes not enough in and of itself. Organizations often depend on employees' identifying with processes.

The dilemma facing managers today is that they cannot motivate their workforces by money and pressure alone because they themselves depend on their employees' active participation. At the same time, the employees' identification with products and processes restricts the organization's ability to change. The factors that create strong identification with an organization prove especially resilient to change when change is needed and can be modified only at the expense of widespread demotivation. It is both a strength and weakness of identification strategies that organizations can change the things that employees identify with only if they are prepared to sustain heavy losses—a problem for which there is no ready solution.

4.3. The Employee Dilemma—When the Focus Is on People

Because organizations have become more open and eliminated the separation between the productive, value-creating core and change-oriented management units, employees now face fundamentally different demands. They are expected to meet the requirements of stability and change at the same time. Two tasks that are in fact contradictory—transforming and stabilizing processes—must be tackled by the same workforce. Management is increasingly requiring workers to ensure a stable value-added process and respond flexibly to market fluctuations, product modifications, and potential technical innovations. Employees are expected to strictly follow rules and instructions while coping effectively with any given situation. The conflicts between stability and change, which used to be handled primarily by supervisors and the staff processing orders, must now be dealt with by workers in production.

Employees are thus confronting contradictory demands to a growing degree. Because paradoxes, contradictions, and "both/and" thinking are now in vogue, employees are increasingly being required to change their fundamental strategies and attitudes. They are now expected to develop a passion for paradoxes, contradictions, both/and approaches, and tweaking processes in order to fulfill the new organizational requirements.

In automotive companies and other corporate groups, lists are circulating that describe the conflicting requirements that employees must fulfill in these new organizational structures. On the one hand, companies are emphasizing the binding nature of target agreements; on the other, they are requiring employees to disregard such agreements in emergencies. On the one hand, companies expect employees to use external services to reduce costs; on the other, they are demanding that, due to the overall profit situation, employees give preference to in-house products. On the one hand, companies are calling on workers to organize their units independently; on the other, they do not want redundant functions to emerge in the company as a whole.

The growing number of dilemmas, conflicting goals, and catch-22s perceived by employees appears to be the price that is being paid for eliminating the separate handling of the requirements of change and stability. The reason employees have the feeling that they are permanently mired in conflicting goals and dilemmas is that contradictory requirements are no longer being met in separate units, but are increasingly cropping up in one and the same organizational area. The reason they have the feeling that they have to focus on preservation *and* change is that there are no longer units specializing in preservation or change. And the reason they have the impression of having to compete and cooperate at the same time is that the managers of the decentralized units are requiring them to simultaneously engage in such contradictory relations with other organizational units. The managers' feeling that they must increasingly allow employees to call the shots even though they as managers are still responsible for processes arises for the same reason.

Mobilizing People as a Resource

At this point one usually finds an "ode to the personnel"—a celebration of human capital and the "new heroes" of the organization. Even if this ode to personnel is described in different ways—as "high-trust relations" that must replace the "low-trust relations" of the Taylorist model (Fox 1974); as a shift from "direct control" to "responsible autonomy" (Friedman 1977); or as a transition from a "type A" to a "type Z" organization (Ouchi 1981)—we must not overlook just how far back the idea of integrating staff goes. Gertraude Krell and Günther Ortmann (Krell/Ortmann 1984) showed that in structural terms, Japan's "company community" (Clark 1981) and the European and U.S. vision of an organizational culture marked by a "we feeling" (Hampden-Turner 1992) do not differ in any fundamental way from the 1920s idea of a "works community" (Kupsch 1926) or the "National Socialist factory community" of the 1930s and 1940s (Höhn 1935).

The message is always the same. What is at stake is a new type of employee. Instead of workers who do their jobs from nine to five and carefully distinguish between their roles as workers and their private lives, managers want loyal "company men" (or women) who can come to the organization's rescue in emergencies even after their working day is done. In speeches, training seminars, and glossy brochures, employees are called upon to invest their entire identity in the organization.

There are two easily understandable reasons for mobilizing human beings as a resource in companies, administrations, armies, and hospitals. First, a complex entity such as a company or an administration can function only if people, with all their subjectivity, can respond flexibly to failures, glitches, and planning errors. The only reason that Frederick Taylor's scientifically planned, strictly hierarchical, specialized organizational form could function was that employees did not rigidly follow rules and shun extra work, but responded flexibly to unexpected eventualities. When a growing number of conflicts and uncertainties reach the core of the organization, flexible responses by "autonomous employees" become increasingly important.

Second, an organization's innovative capacity can be enhanced by mobilizing human beings in all their diversity. The mobilization of individual interests, personal proclivities, and interesting deviations dissolves clarity in organizations. It prevents organizations from becoming entrenched in formalized roles and rules and can contribute to organizational success. It can be advantageous if not all employees have the "organization in their blood," but keep an organization on its toes with all their differences, quirks, and oddities. Sometimes it is precisely the difficult staff members who by constantly breaking rules and disregarding standards help the organization to adapt to changing environmental conditions (Jos/Tompkins/Hays 1989).

Why Employees Do Not Fully Commit Themselves to the Organization

But what would happen if employees were to meet the demand to become more fully committed to the organization? What would happen if a new hire were to take the employment condition of "independent thought and action" seriously? In fact, it would bring every organization to the brink of ruin. Organizations, it can be argued, can survive only because employees leave most of their hopes, problems, and expectations at the door. They can survive only because the employees who were hired on the condition of "independent thought and action" do not do everything they want, but conform to existing expectations.

There is one key factor that distinguishes organizations from families and groups of friends: in families and groups of friends, people often face the expectation of full commitment to the group—that they bring to it all their personal, professional, religious, cultural and athletic hopes and worries. People meet and become attached to each other because of their personalities. People communicate primarily to build relationships without there necessarily being any specific task to carry out.

By contrast, organizations focus on a more or less clearly defined goal. The primary focus in organizations is not to get to know interesting and likeable people, but to link activities and information so as to ensure that pending tasks are carried out. This can involve developing a new railway train or producing components for a power plant. Meeting interesting people is not ruled out, but it is not hard to imagine what would happen if employees gave higher priority to meeting others than to developing a fast train or producing a steam turbine.

With the exception of "greedy institutions" (Coser 1974)—i.e., groups such as sects, revolutionary parties, and communes that seek to control their members in terms of all the role relations in their lives—members of organizations are only partially integrated into organizational structures. They do not need to be fully committed to the organization and are not accountable to them for their roles outside the organization. Managers may regret this arrangement in everyday routines, but generally speaking, the partial integration of members into organizations can be a relief for both organizations and their members. Organizations are freed from having to deal with all aspects of the employees' personalities. In addition, by citing the organization's official purpose, they can keep employees from bringing personal problems to the workplace. Comments such as "I'm sorry, Mr. Jones, but your sexual problems have no place in our company" or "We would ask you, Mrs. Smith, not to make copies of political leaflets during work" do not need to change the general behavior of Mr. Jones or Mrs. Smith. However, they do make the employees aware that they are doing something that has no place in the company.

For employees, being reduced to a specific set of characteristics can be a relief and even liberating. A person's life cannot be completely determined by an organization. That is the main difference between work relations and slavery. Employees can reject, as a violation of their privacy, any attempt by the organization to influence whom they marry, what sport they play, and how many children they have. They can even reject demands by managers that they perform tasks during their working time that are not directly related to the company's business. A male director may attempt to come on to a female employee, and a female director may ask a male employee to wash her car, but all the participating parties know that such conduct is illegal.

In part, the only reason that employees may be able to endure the work that is officially expected of them is that they are not integrated into the organization in terms of all their relations. Probably the only reason people can bear the monotony of assembly line work in the automotive industry or the requirement to offer a friendly "How can I help you?" even to particularly unpleasant customers at a Burger King restaurant is that they can separate the organization from other aspects of their lives.

Focusing on People

To express this idea more clearly, from the organizational perspective, it is irrelevant which person performs an action. Certainly, people are "centers of action," but they are only of marginal interest as individuals. What is important is the work they do in the interests of the organization. Manchester United would continue to exist as a soccer club even if all its players, coaches, team doctors, and goalkeepers were exchanged. A university would continue to function even if it threw out an entire generation of students, dismissed research associates after they had completed their PhDs, and replaced all the established professors with new ones. A company would continue to exist even if the management board resigned, large numbers of workers were dismissed, and a new investor took a majority stake.

The individual players in organizations exert only a limited influence on the rules of the organizational game. Once the rules are established, the game determines the behavior of the individual players. The university plays a central role in organizing the life of its professors and students. The same applies to ministerial bureaucracies. From this perspective, it is not company management that controls the company, but the company that controls the employees so that it can function.

Former General Electric CEO Jack Welch was given the unflattering nickname "Neutron Jack" because of his ruthless personnel policy. Like a neutron bomb, he "destroyed" the unsuitable, antagonistic employees through the pressure he applied, while leaving the corporate infrastructure in place (e.g., processes, computer programs, organizational structures) and filling it with acceptable employees. Despite the cruelty and cynicism expressed by his nickname, it reveals a deeper organizational insight. An organization continues to exist even if the staff is replaced. And even if Jack Welch had fallen victim to a neutron bomb that he, his inferiors, or GE's largest shareholders ignited, it would not have spelled the end of GE.

The individual is only of minor importance to the organization. The primary goal of organizations is not to use all of their employees' capabilities, but to coordinate communication. The main components of organizations are not individuals, but communicated messages. Coordination within organizations depends above all on formalized rules, not on the personal characteristics of individuals. This is what distinguishes organizations from families, groups of friends, people standing on line, or a group of regulars lined up at a bar.

This fact explains a frequently observed organizational strategy. According to Cornelius Castoriadis (Castoriadis 1987), management has an interest in making sure that each employee is interchangeable in terms of her function. The organization must "maintain all processes vital for its survival," regardless of whether the worker Smith dies from a heart attack, wins the lottery and no longer has to work, or starts her own company. It must ensure that there are "always several providers of each required behavior."

Organizations are characterized by the fact that they abstract from the individual interests of their employees. In signing an employment contract, new employees agree to place their interests on the back burner and to accept the rules of the organization. The formalization of positions, roles, and rules in organizations ensures that, despite the very different personal interests, there is reliability regarding the decisions in the organization.

When organizations reintroduce the human factor into their organizational policy, it may have an ideological significance, but it in fact amounts to a highly restricted reintroduction of something that had previously been eliminated. Through human-centric models, psychologically oriented communication training, and company celebrations, organizations are ultimately only attempting to readmit, in small, easily manageable doses, the human factor that they actually tend to exclude (Luhmann 2000, 89).

Corporates versus Cowboys—a Dilemma

The problem facing organizations is that they need to suppress local interests and personal wishes but also to factor in such interests. According to management consultant Rosabeth M. Kanter (Kanter 1989), organizations communicate to their employees that as "bureaucrats" and "corporates," they must adapt to the organization's prescribed rules and structures, but as "cowboys" and "cowgirls," they must mix things up with their individualism.

If a holding company that owns a major Dutch industrial enterprise demands an entrepreneurial mindset from the directors of the enterprise's individual divisions, the holding company would act paradoxically if it then required the directors to consider the holding company's managerial interests. If Deutsche Bank's London headquarters hires a stockbroker and pays her a high salary because of her strong, independent personality, it, too, would act paradoxically if at the same time it demanded her unconditional identification with the bank's objectives. Ultimately, such organizations communicate conflicting requirements: on the one hand, the demand that employees disregard formalized roles, structures, and identities; on the other hand, that they meet such demands. They expect employees to adhere to the existing structures and support the company's objectives while at the same time asking them to break the rules as entrepreneurially minded individuals.

Organizational management thus faces a dilemma. On the one hand, the organization can benefit if employees become fully involved. Despite formalized rules and roles, such participation leads to a beneficial working environment. On the other hand, organizations are dependent on restricting and suppressing local interests because this is the only way the basic principle of the organization in the form of formalized rules and roles can be upheld.

4.4. The Dilemma of Communication— the Strengths and Weaknesses of Discussion

According to (married) South African/American consultants Patricia McLagan and Christo Nel (McLagan/Nel 1995), an era of communication and participation is dawning in organizations. Among managers, organizational consultants, and scholars, there is widespread agreement that comprehensive change processes cannot be imposed from above, but need to be negotiated through intense communication.

The Advantages of Linguistic Communication

When management consultants speak enthusiastically about an era of participation and communication, they are simplifying matters in significant ways. Participation and communication have always been hallmarks of organizations, and even the oft demonized Taylorist organization was no exception in this regard. Hierarchical instructions, cash payments, tasks specified by machines—all entail communication. Even employees who do their jobs in complete isolation participate and are involved. Were an organization to dispense with communication and participation entirely, it would not be an organization at all. Its decisions would exist randomly in space and could not be interconnected.

When authors refer to communication and participation, they have a special form of communication in mind—the language-based communication between the organization's employees. With terms such as discursive organization, participatory organizational management, and consensual management, they emphasize the greater importance of this linguistic communication. The idea is that communicative change strategies that rely on negotiation and communication are much more successful than technocratic, hierarchically coordinated change processes.

These reflections in management literature have much in common with the observations of philosopher Jürgen Habermas. In his theory of communicative action (Habermas 1984), Habermas calls for actions to be coordinated through acts of communication. A prerequisite for these communication processes is a common pool of cultural knowledge and a core collection of overarching standards.

Managing organizations via communication and negotiation has obvious advantages. In their attempt to solve a problem, organizations mobilize the views of many employees and set them in relation to each other. By weighing different views, organizations hope to find the best approach and thus to optimize the quality of the solution. At the same time, through communication and negotiation, the motivation and control problems faced by management are reduced. The idea is that, by broadly involving employees, organizations can recruit them as supporters of change. One mantra often heard in organizational development is that the affected parties should be made into participants. This lessens the fear of change and allows solutions to be rapidly implemented. Employees choose a certain method for solving a problem because they have reached agreement with all participants concerning the path forward, not because they have been forced to do so by orders or by market processes. The hope is that, as a result, motivation and control measures will not be necessary.

Communication Overload

This demand for language-based communication in companies is interesting because the social systems that rely exclusively on linguistic communication and negotiation are not particularly good at dealing with complex tasks. We need only think of the family, in which all coordination processes—from planning weddings and baptisms to taking care of grandparents and doing work in the yard—are taken care of primarily through linguistic communication. In other words, in the modern family, the cases in which cash payments ("I pay my children to clean the bathroom"), hierarchical orders ("My grandparents need to shut up because I'm the boss here") and references to scientific truths ("In our family women drive because it is scientifically proven that men are the worst drivers") are used as a means of communication are probably more of an exception than a rule.

Linguistic communication within the family has proved its value for low-complexity tasks. The family is a relatively successful system when it comes to cleaning the house, stabilizing the emotional lives of its male members, and raising children. However, through the course of its evolution, the family system—with its basis in oral communication—has not caught on for comprehensive production processes or the satisfaction of complex customer needs. The majority of family-run businesses function like families, with all their strengths and weaknesses, only at the executive level. Otherwise they function like organizations.

Organizations that use the communication model of the family and coordinate processes primarily through oral communication quickly fall prey to communication overload. It is, for example, perfectly understandable why in a medium-sized software company, in response to a communication campaign by management, employees might also want to discuss "who should do less talking with each other." Organizations can be compared to the human brain. Human beings also restrict the communication between neurons and (fortunately!) use only a fraction of their brain capacity. If they did not, they might risk an epileptic seizure.

The Strengths of Hierarchy

There is a tried-and-true mechanism for performing complex tasks and simultaneously protecting the organization from linguistic communication overload: the hierarchy. Its development is interesting because many areas of modern society get by without any formal hierarchy, including not only individual groups, but also the economy, science, culture, sports, and politics. As a rule, there is no longer an emperor, king, or pope to determine whether a product sells or flops, whether a finding is true or false, whether a painting is beautiful or ugly, whether the Mets win the World Series, or whether a political party remains in power or is ousted.

However, hierarchies still appear to be popular as central control mechanisms in organizations. Despite all the fashionable demands to flatten hierarchies, to eliminate hierarchical barriers, and to smash hierarchical structures, it is difficult to imagine an organization without a hierarchy today. Organizations that operate in various spheres of society, such as companies, universities, art museums, sports clubs, and political parties, are dependent on hierarchies. Even the plucky attempts by self-administrating factories, reform universities, decentralized art initiatives, soccer clubs, and grassroots political initiatives to get by without this coordination mechanism run the risk of failure once tasks grow more complex.

The strengths of hierarchies as coordination mechanisms have to do with the fact that that they do not eliminate linguistic communication entirely, but greatly reduce the need for it. As Talcott Parsons (Parsons 1965) pointed out, hierarchies efficiently separate the various levels of a company, an association, or an administration and permit only well-defined oral communication (the so-called lines of command, reporting, and communication channels). They effectively protect each level from becoming overwhelmed with the communication needs of the other levels by defining exactly which linguistic communication is considered relevant.

Hierarchies thus produce modularity. Modularity means that subsystems are independent in various ways. The advantage is that not everything that happens in one module affects the entire organization. A lot can happen in one subsystem without it immediately impacting the other subsystems. Only at a few defined interfaces does the behavior of one module become relevant to another.

These modules are the divisions and subdivisions of a company. In many areas of work, top management, business divisions, and subdivisions are independent. They do not need to account to each other for all their actions. It is of little interest to the other modules, even to the next one up in the hierarchy, whether one business division hires a new employee or launches a new marketing campaign. The only places where communication is permitted between modules that occupy the same hierarchical level or between modules of different levels are those defined by top management.

Herbert A. Simon (Simon 1962) showed that this separation of levels enables organizations to handle a great deal of complexity. As part of the hierarchical structure, an organization is divided into subsystems that are in turn divided into additional subsystems. The density of communication within the individual subsystems is greater than that between the subsystems. It is within these subsystems that solutions are developed and made available to the organization as a whole.

This brings several advantages. First, it is possible to master complex tasks. For such tasks, the organization does not need to develop a comprehensive solution, but can avail itself of partial solutions. Let us assume, for example, that the telecommunication networks division of a U.S. electronics group plans to launch a new telephone switching system. It would totally overwhelm employees if they were forced to develop the solution in a large consensus-based group. In the real world, the task of developing switching centers is divided into many subprojects in which independent subsystems develop a series of partial solutions. This approach is effective because the hierarchical mechanism successfully separates the subsystems and permits only selective communication between them.

Second, it is not necessary for a hierarchical organization to start from scratch when confronting new challenges. It can use the partial solutions it has already developed. When tackling the telephone switching system, for example, it can draw on the various, previously developed partial solutions and use existing subsystems that work well together. The partial solutions can be interconnected in flexible ways.

Third, partial solutions can be saved for later use, even if the company does not manage to complete the overall solution. Perhaps competition from the Internet keeps the company from developing the telephone switching system to the point where it can be marketed. If the product had been conceived as an all-encompassing solution, the project could easily result in a commercial disaster: the company would stand to lose hundreds of millions of dollars and waste the labor of thousands of people. However, because the product has been conceived as many partial solutions, it is possible to use these components for other purposes.

Herbert A. Simon (Simon 1962, 470ff.) told the parable of two watchmakers named Hora and Tempus to illustrate the strengths of hierarchies. Both of these fictitious watchmakers made fine Swiss pocket watches. Both were highly regarded by customers at home and abroad and in both of their workshops the phones were ringing off the hook. However, while Hora's business flourished, Tempus grew poorer and poorer and finally lost his shop. What was the reason?

The watches made by the two precision craftsmen consisted of thousands of parts. Because of the way Tempus designed his watch, he needed to assemble it in a single operation. If he was forced to put down an unfinished watch because a valued customer called him to place a new order, the watch fell into a thousand pieces and Tempus had to start assembling it all over again. The more the customers liked his watches, the more calls he received and the more difficult it became for him to find enough time to make his watches. In other words, as his market presence grew, he became less efficient.

Hora's watches were not any less complex than those made by Tempus, but he had designed them so that he could put them together from one hundred subassemblies of about ten elements each. Ten of these subassemblies formed one larger subassembly. Ten larger subassemblies made up the entire watch. Hence, when Hora put aside a partially assembled watch to talk on the phone, he lost only a small part of his work and was able to assemble his watch in only a fraction of the working time required by Tempus.

Negotiation versus Hierarchy

Organizations face a dilemma. On the one hand, management needs to mobilize linguistic communication within organizations because communication mechanisms such as "hierarchy" and "market" entail rigid processes. Ongoing communication between all employees would appear to be the only way to meet the requirements of change. On the other hand, organizations need to reduce the possibility of communication through hierarchical structures in order to cope with complex tasks. If they do not, employees become worn down by the stress of communicating when they attempt to solve larger problems.

The establishment of project groups is one popular trick used by organizations to solve this dilemma. Parallel to hierarchical organizational structures, individuals are assembled from different departments and hierarchical levels—as well as from outside the organization—to carry out short-term projects. This is done in the hope that information can be collected from the various units and the search for solutions will be marked by a high degree of consensus and responsibility in the individual units.

Thanks to the project groups, short-term structures are formed that are decoupled from the hierarchy but are integrated into the overall hierarchical organization. Decision-making within project groups is usually based on consensual negotiations and agreements, but the results achieved by the project groups can be implemented hierarchically. In the project group itself it is not possible for project managers to make decisions by playing the "boss" card. However, project groups can always fall back on the dominant hierarchical structure to resolve decision-making difficulties.

Project-based organization does not resolve the dilemma between hierarchy and linguistic communication. It merely shifts it to the project groups. The overall organization is relieved of a contradiction at the expense of the group's members. Traditionally, the members of the project group face the predicament of "dual responsibilities." On the one hand, they are responsible for ensuring that, via communication and negotiation, the project group achieves its desired goal; on the other, they are accountable to their hierarchically organized units.

The interests of the project group and the units from which the members come not only differ, but are often inherently contradictory. Because of their dual responsibilities, members of the group often feel they must fulfill opposing demands. On the one hand, in a project group established to introduce group work in a company, the representative of the manufacturing unit must ensure that group work is indeed introduced. On the other, she must represent her unit's interests. In a project group formed to implement a new IT system, an employee from the order management department must see to it that a new computer system is indeed up and running by the end of the project. On the other hand, she must prevent order management from losing influence because of the new system.

The frequent problems encountered in project work are largely the result of these conflicting demands. Project managers despair because of their lack of authority. Project groups are worn down by hierarchies. The project groups merely reflect the overall hierarchical structure, and their members mutually block each other. Instead of dissolving the organizational structures, the project group merely reproduces them.

In summary, it can be said that the dilemma between supporting and selectively preventing communication cannot be solved by project-based organization. It is only delegated to specialized work units. It may therefore appear to be resolved from the perspective of top management, but it has not disappeared from the organization.

4.5. The Dilemma of Self-Organization— When Self-Organization Is Determined by Organization by Others

The promotion of employee self-organization is touted as a key factor for the success of innovative organizations. But although the question of how to implement self-organization is often discussed, its underlying problems are rarely examined in detail. Many proponents of self-organization seem to assume that self-organized structures emerge automatically if employees are given the appropriate freedoms (e.g. Laloux 2014, 61ff.). The argument for self-organization would seem to prohibit too much structuring of the self-organized unit by managers, because otherwise it would not be self-organization.

Self-organization is one of the management concepts that are currently difficult to criticize because it evokes so many positive associations. However, it is worth noting that self-organization is welcomed more enthusiastically by managers than by the self-organizing employees themselves. This is to a certain extent understandable. After all, at first glance, it is the managers, not the employees, who are relieved of work by the self-organization of subordinate units. As a result, in many cases employees are gently forced into self-organization, along the lines of: when children do not want to jump into a pool of cold water, they have to be pushed in instead. Parents may offer a few words of advice on how their kids should move their arms and kick once they are in the water, but what they do there is generally left to them.

Traditional Structures Resulting from Self-Organization

The central questions are: What work and decision-making processes do the self-organizing groups that are pushed into cold water develop when left to their own devices? Does self-organization lead to new, more innovative, and more flexible structures? Are self-organized structures fundamentally different from structures organized by others?

Probably not. The dilemma of self-organization is that self-organizing units are primarily oriented toward familiar structures organized by others in the organization. Alfred Kieser (Kieser 1994) has pointed out that in the process of self-organization, structures are reproduced with which the participants are familiar. In most organizations these are the structures that were already known before the official introduction of self-organization. Or they are the diverse structures surrounding the "islands of official self-organization."

In this context, the ideal organizational form would appear to be the fractal structures that have become quite a fetish these days but are in fact more frequently found in journals than in organizational practice. Fractal organizations consist of collections of self-organizing units that, in terms of their basic elements, have formed very similar structures. The tragedy of this management concept is that it rarely appears relevant in areas in which it is supposed to work, but has an impact on others where management does not want to use it. The concept of the fractal organization is invoked as a new miracle cure, but structurally identical fractals form where there is least use for them—namely, in the self-organization process that is actually meant to create innovations.

This self-organized reproduction of familiar structural patterns is not all that surprising: the success and survival of organizations and organizational units often depends on the fact that organizations incorporate the institutional elements of the outside world into their own structures. Just as organizations adapt, at least verbally, to the principles of their own environments, so, too, do organizational units partially adapt to the structures, language, and behavior of the entire organization. If the new managing director mentions the establishment of a "new mindset," managers and employees will also suddenly begin discussing the need for "a new mindset"—even though no official memo has circulated requiring the use of this terminology.

Any company that has tried to introduce group work is probably familiar with the problem of self-organization that is oriented to organization outside the group. By introducing group work, the organization may hope that collective, self-organized order planning and processing will function better than management by a foremen or supervisor. But what inevitably happens is that the production group selects (though now in a self-organized manner) a supervisor who handles order planning. In this way, the group spokesperson, who in true group work would only play the role of moderator, becomes an informal supervisor. This process is not surprising because when it self-organizes, the group draws on what it already knows: the previous form of work organization and the hierarchical methods of management that determine other processes in the company.

The Alienating Effect of Organization by Others

Despite the idealization of self-organized processes, self-organized change can be the wrong path to take for an organization. Innovations can sometimes be achieved more quickly within the framework of organization by others than in the self-organized processes in which the structures of the next higher levels are unconsciously reproduced.

From this perspective, consultations with experts bring the advantage of offering a structure that is often completely foreign to the organization. Even if the objection can be raised that in many cases the structure that is offered is only a slightly modified version of a structure from another consulting project, it still performs an important function. External impetus is introduced into the organization and must be integrated into the mechanisms of the self-organized system.

Organizations face a dilemma. On the one hand, the mechanisms of self-organized systems are important for mobilizing problem-solving capacities within the organization. On the other hand, managers need external organization to introduce new, unfamiliar solutions.

4.6. The Dilemma of Reserves— the Demand for Self-Obstruction

The days are long gone when the brave crusaders against organizational waste and buffers could count on undivided support in organizations. For a time, the promoters of lean companies, lean associations, and lean public authorities were able to profit from the popular practice of denouncing reserves of materials and staff as unnecessary cost drivers. Organizational buffers, reserves, and flab were seen mainly as an expression of inefficiency. Staff reserves and excess stocks of material and intermediary products were considered a sign of waste and inefficient production. It was claimed that these buffers and reserves served only to conceal planning errors, machine breakdowns, and technical difficulties.

The commitment of resources and efforts to activities not directly related to work processes was criticized as wasteful. The guiding principle of Japanese automaker Toyota—"Act in a goal-directed and practical manner and avoid the unnecessary"—was embraced by many managers who had great respect for the successes of Japanese industry. When lean management pioneer Daniel T. Jones complained that it was highly wasteful for components to be transported seven miles through a factory in four months' time only to be assembled in four to five hours, many managers sympathized with his view. As part of this lean ideology, it became popular to prescribe radical "starvation diets" to organizations in the form of hiring freezes and cost-cutting measures. Process orientation was promoted as the method of choice for reducing waste and eliminating buffers. A zero-error principle was demanded for all organizational processes as another waste-avoidance strategy. Processes were connected in fixed ways without the use of reserves or wiggle room so that companies could produce as efficiently as possible.

The Efficiency of Inefficiency—the Use of Buffers

However, no sooner was this principle established than those thinkers who had championed lean principles and the elimination of buffers and reserves began confronting stiff headwinds. Many of the organizations that had systematically focused on lean management and streamlining found that by radically reducing organizational reserves, they were causing considerable problems for themselves: their organizations had become error-prone. There were no reserves available for stressful situations. Conflicts and disturbances could no longer be mitigated, and flexibility was lost. Instead of the hoped-for reduction of complexity through lean principles, there was increased complexity due to overload, stress, and conflict. Every minor disturbance—e.g., a truckers' strike in France, machinery problems in a supplier's plant, workforce dissatisfaction—had a direct impact on the company. The seemingly insignificant software problems experienced by a supplier of door and trunk locks had the potential to stop assembly lines in an automotive group.

The view that buffers and reserves are wasted rationalization opportunities is based on the assumption that the world is a relatively stable place. The negative evaluation of buffers and reserves presupposes the idea that organizations exist in a relatively stable, conflict-free environment in which all requirements can be incorporated into the traditional, strictly rationalized organization of work.

In increasingly turbulent environments, however, many managers eventually realized that buffers and reserves—the "slack" of the organization—were not always wasted resources, but could perform important organizational functions. They recognized that while small organizational buffers did not serve the actual purpose of the organization's work and were not always required by the organization, they nonetheless represented a crucial resource for future requirements. [20]

---

20 This debate on the benefits of buffers, which has now reached organizational practitioners, goes back to Cyert and March (Cyert/March 1963, 33ff.). The reflections by Cyert and March were modified and expanded on by Karl E. Weick (Weick 1976), who made a distinction between "tight couplings" and "loose couplings." Building on Cyert and March, other authors have focused on the various advantages of slack. James March (March 1988), for example, points to the role of buffers in conflict avoidance. In connection with Cyert and March (Cyert/March 1963, 278–79), Granovetter (Granovetter 1973) and Nonaka and Takeuchi (Nonaka/Takeuchi 1995), among others, explore the role of buffers in innovation management. What is important to me is not a continuance of the unproductive back and forth between "slack is good" and "slack is bad." It would hardly be original to respond to a praise of waste by criticizing waste from the perspective of lean management. In connection with Weick's work, it seems more revealing to conceptualize the slack problem as a dilemma that cannot be resolved simply by the demand that "we need both slack and streamlined structures."

First, these reserves can help prevent conflicts because they relieve organizations of the need to precisely synchronize all goals internally. In addition, conflicts are minimized because organizations can draw on surplus resources that satisfy different, even contradictory, needs. Large temporary storage facilities prevent conflicts from arising between the production and sales departments. Sizable financial reserves reduce the risk that simultaneous claims from different departments cannot be met.

A second function of organizational buffers is that they prepare the organization for overload situations. It may make sense for a company to employ product developers even in times when product innovation is not on the agenda. Over the long term it may also be smart for a production company to employ a precision welder who can solve complex errors even if her skills are rarely required by the individual departments.

A third reason for creating reserves and buffers is to prevent errors from having a direct effect on the organization. For some companies it can make sense for employees to be able to stop the assembly line immediately when a small product defect is discovered. However, it may be more important for others to design a production system with buffers that can withstand a large number of errors. Companies must prevent every incident in normal routines from becoming crises. Through buffers and reserves, "loosely coupled" companies become tolerant of errors.

Fourth, reserves can fulfill key functions in organizations. A company that has perfectly adapted to the market situation and focused its entire organization on efficiently serving market niches can face a fundamental problem if the market situation changes. It will not have any surplus resources on hand to effectively realign itself to the new situations. Certainly, thanks to the elimination of resources, buffers, and flab, such an organization has effectively adapted to the existing situation, but it is no longer adaptable to new ones.

This means that the organization must have human, financial, material, and intellectual resources that it can draw on at short notice, especially in situations that require great adaptability. Maneuvering room is required to survive a crisis. Surplus resources are needed to be efficient. Such buffers can create the necessary scope for experimentation. They can provide a decisive resource for innovation and change. Reserves within the organization represent the excess time and resources needed to try out new things.

Organizations create for themselves "reservations of waste" and protect these reservations against the requirements of change. They hope that the freed-up workers will spend their time on something useful. The organization that has pursued these policies most single-mindedly is probably the U.S. corporation 3M, which operates in a variety of markets, such as adhesives, personal care, and telecommunications. In its "Rules of Innovation Management," 3M proposed giving employees sufficient freedoms, eliminating bans on independent thinking, and supporting risky ventures. Employees were officially allowed to spend 15 percent of their work time on projects outside their areas of responsibility.

The redundancies that are often complained about in organizations create scope for development, a grasp of the big picture, and internal competition, thus providing opportunities for learning. If there were no duplications or overlaps, organizations would find it difficult to identify alternative routes.

Rejoicing in Mistakes—in Praise of Waste

If an organization's ability to accept its mistakes is celebrated as an organizational strength, a positive view of buffers, reserves, and slack is revealed. IBM founder Thomas Watson is quoted as saying, "The fastest way to succeed is to double your rate of failure." Arguing that errors should be accepted, Watson told an unusual anecdote about one of his junior executives who had lost ten million dollars on a risky project. According to Watson, he summoned the young man to his office, where, trembling in fear, the young man said, "I guess you want my resignation." But Watson dismissed the offer indignantly, saying, "You can't be serious. We just spent ten million dollars educating you."

Management consultants Tom Peters and Robert Waterman (Peters/Waterman 1982) created a management philosophy out of an acceptance of errors. Their slogan might be expressed as, "Make as many mistakes as you want, but do so with intellect, style, and grace." In their productive search for excellence, they argued that a high tolerance of failures was the only way to create an innovative work environment. They believed this tolerance was the secret of many companies' success.

Against a Renaissance of Buffers—
the Dilemma of Self-Obstruction

It is perfectly understandable why, after a period of excessive lean management and organizational anorexia, the idea of organizational buffers is experiencing a renaissance. One is reminded of the person who, after several weeks on a radical diet, rediscovers the benefits of a certain amount of body fat. Companies that have lost the freedom to experiment as a result of their starvation diets build up reserves once again in order to have the resources for innovation. Firms that have amputated entire business segments in order to concentrate on their core business discover that they have lost attractive parts of their organization, parts that are in fact crucial to this core business. They begin making acquisitions again—often in the markets where they previously sold divisions.

However, this strong emphasis on the benefits of buffers and reserves as a means to minimize conflicts, promote a tolerance of errors, prepare for overload, and advance innovation should not distract us from the fact that buffers and reserves are associated with an organizational dilemma. Ultimately, buffers and reserves result from a non-optimal use of resources. Using them, organizations make processes more complex. Organizations do not take the most direct route from A to B, but consciously use a winding route and place additional obstacles in their way—all in the hope that by making things more difficult, they will be forced to take new paths and possibly generate new ideas (Weick 1979).

The creation of reserves and buffers leads to a paradoxical situation. In contrast to the logic of the zero-error principle promoted in many fields, here organizations call on their employees to delight in experimentation and risk failure. The underlying assumption is that, when employees try out something new, they will (and should be allowed to) make mistakes. These mistakes are no longer seen as preventable losses, but as an opportunity to learn and change. They allow organizations to adapt to turbulent environments (Peters 1994).

Ultimately, employees might see the use of reserves as an invitation to organizational self-obstruction. The organization makes processes more complex and prevents rationally organized production. Organizations accept a degree of organizational carelessness in the hope that they will have reserves at their disposal if they are suddenly confronted with new requirements. Organizations put on flab and allow redundancies in the hope that employees will use these resources for innovation, added flexibility, and change. In other words, organizations consciously risk a "sloppy" organization of work and decision-making processes so that they will have the potential to deal with problems in the future (Cyert/March 1963). Managers sacrifice an organization that is optimally adapted to current requirements in the hope that through the resulting buffers they will be prepared for different future demands (Weick 1979).

The creation of reserves and the tolerance of errors can be likened to management introducing coffee and tea breaks so as to allow employees to meet informally without any pressure from above and without any predefined goals—all in the hope that employees will use the opportunity to create innovations. It is as if, in order to facilitate innovation and change, managers were to equip buildings with long hallways, spacious, slow, error-prone elevators, and a small number of oft-clogged toilets, all in the hope that employees will take advantage of the resulting interactions with colleagues for creative processes (Luhmann 2000, 358).

Organizations face a dilemma. This organizational self-obstruction, caused by sloppiness and carelessness, *can* lead to reserves being used to develop innovations; however, this need not be the case. The problem is that the meaningful use of reserves cannot be prescribed organizationally. If it were possible to precisely control the use of buffers and reserves, they would no longer be buffers and reserves, but aspects of a highly streamlined organization. Leaders of an organization can hope that employees will use buffers for something meaningful, but they do not have effective ways to control it. In organizations, reserves of money, time, and materials can be used to make the organization more innovative, or they can be used to hide mistakes and misconduct. It is indeed possible that the coffee breaks, the long corridors, the spacious, slow elevators, and the small number of toilets will make the employees more creative. However, it is also possible that they will lead to a situation in which employees rush from coffee break to coffee break, drum their fingers impatiently on elevator walls, develop a fear of going out into the long corridors alone, and have nightmarish experiences in the bathrooms.

4.7. The Learning Dilemma—When Organizations Fall Victim to Successful Learning

Organizational learning is a high priority for the management teams of many organizations. A large number of managers assume that the ability to adapt and learn is a basic criterion for organizational success and that organizations that successfully complete a learning process derive from it ways to learn even more effectively in the future. The prevailing view is that through continuous learning, organizations always get better at learning.

The basic assumption is that an organization that learns and changes successfully today is well equipped for future challenges; that learning lays a solid foundation for the future.

The Failure of Successful Organizations

In practice, often the opposite can be observed. We need only look at the organizations that have failed because of a successful change, learning, or innovation process, or that have experienced serious difficulties, at least over the long term, because of successful change and learning. Of the ten most innovative and successful British companies in the 1980s, four went bankrupt within the space of just a few years, and only three turned a profit after they were lauded in public for their success. Almost half of the companies on the 1984 list of the five hundred largest international corporations no longer existed roughly ten years later. Of the forty-three "excellent companies" that were praised by former McKinsey consultants Tom Peters and Robert Waterman and which—thanks primarily to the two consultants' book—were ranked among the best-managed companies in the United States, almost half faced serious problems five years later or suffered from a weak position in the market. Exemplary companies such Atari and Revlon were teetering on the brink of bankruptcy. Even the "excellent" German companies recognized in the preface to the German edition of the consultants' book, which were evidently taken from McKinsey's client reference list, were plagued by massive problems not long afterward. The praise that the McKinsey consultants showered on Enron as an industry pioneer proved particularly embarrassing: shortly after the book appeared, the company filed for bankruptcy, revealing that its supposed success was based exclusively on the illegal manipulation of balance sheets.[21]

The neglect of change processes and learning is often cited as the reason for the sudden demise of such companies. According to Günter Conrad, former director of Andersen Consulting (which went bankrupt itself), the failed directors of formerly successful companies should resign for neglecting to make learning and change part of their corporate cultures (Gloger/Groothius 1994, 54). However, what is deliberately overlooked is the fact that successful learning and change are partially to blame when companies neglect learning and change.

It is fascinating to observe how companies that have learned and changed successfully can become particularly resistant to learning and

---

21 To the best of my knowledge, the problems besetting the companies listed by Peters and Waterman were first described in an article in *Business Week* dated April 16, 1984 and cited in various business books (Pascale 1990). On the "dual reality" at Enron, see (Kühl 2005). The stories of success and failure were of course fictitious. There is a great deal of overlap between the "excellent companies" mentioned by Peters and Waterman and McKinsey's corporate reference list.

change in the future. In many of these companies, it is precisely the establishment of learning and change in corporate cultures that appears to contribute to problems later on. Once again, we seem to be dealing with a paradoxical situation: the reason for failure lies in success.

How is it possible for successful organizational learning and change to lead to failure?

For the most part, organizational knowledge—resulting from successful learning processes—is not stored in the minds of employees. If this were the case, it would be available only for a short time and would disappear once the individual employee left the organization. At best, individual knowledge-acquisition processes represent learning and knowledge *in* organizations, not learning and knowledge acquisition *by* organizations.

Organizational knowledge establishes itself in the form of sets of rules. Because organizations, unlike people, do not have brains that would enable them to learn, they retain the results of successful learning and change processes in standards, procedures, and parameters. Once this happens, organizational knowledge exists in organizational guidelines, routines, job descriptions, computer programs, and quality manuals (Hedberg 1981).

Organizational researchers Richard R. Nelson and Sidney G. Winter (Nelson/Winter 1982) showed that as a result of successful learning processes, positive-seeming "comps"—i.e., routines—are selected that store knowledge in organizations. In the form of production methods, organization plans, job descriptions, procedural guidelines, and technical programs, this knowledge guides all the actions of the organization. The comps are similar to genetic material—after all, genes also store the knowledge that causes amoebas, monkeys, human beings, etc., to grow.

Of course, these rules are meaningless without people. It is ultimately people who formulate and document the knowledge relevant to the organization. However, this process is not dependent on a specific individual. While it is true that a specific person needs to ensure that quality standards are maintained in the production of window frames, it is largely irrelevant who that person is.

One example of an organizational learning process that is not dependent on people is the introduction of group work in a manufacturing plant. Due to the growing requirements of change, management might consider moving away from assembly-line production. Typically, in cooperation with workers, it would then develop a production structure that transfers responsibility for one area of work to a set team. As long as the knowledge relating to the new team-based production organization exists only in the minds of managers or employees, the result is not an organizational learning and knowledge process, but an *accumulation* of individual learning and knowledge processes. An organizational learning and knowledge process arises only if the new structures, rules, and cultures continue to exist after the employees and managers originally involved have left the company.

Hence, learning and knowledge processes result in entrenched structures, rules, and cultures. Due to successful learning and change, structures that are legitimized by success are established for the long term. The questioning and transformation of structures in organizations ultimately leads to the creation of new structures that for their part create immobility and permanence.

Competency Traps and Learning Dead Ends

However, in view the fact that the world can be a completely different place tomorrow than it is today, all the things that an organization commits itself to today can pose a risk. The structures and routines established by successful learning and change are successful only as long as the general conditions faced by the organization do not change in any fundamental way. If the environment does change, the structures that were established by success can lead to failure. It is precisely the successes perceived by organizations that can keep them from realizing that a more fundamental transformation of organizational structures may be necessary. Put differently, successful crisis resolution, organizational change, and collective learning can lead to disaster if the acquired knowledge at some point becomes useless.

Learning processes can cause organizations to become caught in competency traps. Management may be tempted to continue a successful learning process or to refine existing ones. Once successful rules and routines have been introduced, organizations usually try to increase efficiency by refining existing routines. The more the organization draws on these rules and routines, the better it becomes at applying such rules. As a result, the organization convinces itself that it is on the right track. Such convictions lead to a self-reinforcing learning process, and the organization ultimately settles for solutions that are non-optimal over the long term (March 1994, 96–97).

It is becoming increasingly clear that most organizations have no basic problem with optimization processes that take place in many small steps. Through continuous improvement processes, Kaizen programs, learning centers, and quality circles, autonomously acting working groups track down and correct errors. Under such conditions, the existing rules do not need to be fundamentally changed, and employees immediately see the successes of their learning processes. However, such daily optimizations based on short-term learning processes can prevent more basic learning processes from taking place: organizations refine and optimize their existing structures so intensively that structures no longer undergo fundamental change as a result of renewed learning.

The problem of successful learning and organizational change can be attributed to one basic principle of organizations: organizational decisions create the framework for future decisions. All subsequent learning is based on these existing structures. Organizational memory, consisting of established routines and values, influences the new knowledge that can be learned down the line.

There are many examples of how organizations fall into such competency traps and learning dead ends. A mail order company might develop and perfect an accounting program itself. Because of its financial and human resource investments, it increasingly believes it has taken the right path. At the same time, it creates obstacles for itself that can prevent the shift to a new, more innovative program. The short-term gains in efficiency that can be achieved by perfecting the self-coded accounting program make the organization blind to the possible long-term gains in efficiency that can be achieved by switching to another standard program.

At first glance, management might believe it is increasing efficiency by successfully introducing a highly automated warehousing system. This warehousing system not only improves delivery quality, but also enhances the company's reputation because it is admired by customers and described as innovative in the business press. However, as the successfully introduced system becomes more closely associated with the company's identity, it becomes difficult for the company to replace it if the need suddenly arises for a more flexible, cost-effective solution.

Another example is the field of nuclear energy. In the 1950s the energy industry did not initially have a strong interest in using nuclear energy to generate electricity. It only explored the technical feasibility of nuclear energy due to political pressure. Eventually the major energy companies committed themselves to nuclear energy and began expanding it so heavily that they lost sight of its dangers and neglected alternative means of energy production.

Some companies end up in these learning cul-de-sacs several times in a row without seeming to know how to resolve the problem. "If Siemens only knew what Siemens knows"—uttered with a sigh—was once a part of Siemens' corporate culture. As revealing as this saying is, though, it conceals the fact that the problem at Siemens can also be seen as a problem of too much knowledge. According to the company's own reports, the telecommunications division "slept through" the development of fax machines and Internet data transmission because management had previously introduced successful learning processes in these application fields. Siemens experimented early on with fax machines and could easily have marketed them, but because the corporation was successful in developing its telex business and learning processes were intensified there, it left the fax business to other companies. The same thing occurred in the development of exchanges for telephone networks. Siemens—one of the market leaders in this field—put a great deal of energy into developing switching technology and digitizing its switching centers. Under the catchy name "asynchronous transfer mode," it even developed a technology that allowed data and voice to be transferred along the same line. Because of the intensive learning efforts in this area, though, management long overlooked the fact that it had become much easier to transmit data and voice via the Internet. Siemens' dominant market position was increasingly jeopardized. The problem, noted Volker Jung, a management board member at the time, was that successful products had been promoted for far too long. Siemens chronically failed to recognize the move to new technologies. There are probably quite a few Siemens managers who, in retrospect, now wish that Siemens had known what Siemens knew.

With reference to this problem, economist John Maynard Keynes once claimed that what was difficult for people was not taking up new ideas, but forgetting old ones. In this connection Karl Weick (Weick 1979) pointed to the danger of memories that were excessively good. Weick was of the opinion that few organizations failed because they had forgotten something important. It was much more likely for them to fail because they remembered too much for too long a time due to past successes in learning and change and because they continued doing things in the same way they had always done them with great success.

In organizations, the scope of action can be restricted by the routines that, due to their success, have become lodged in an organization's memory. Whenever organizations adapt to situations by learning, they simultaneously lose some of the "mental" resources that enable them to identify the need for new learning processes. They sacrifice future adaptability for current adaptation. The tragedy of a memory trained by success is that it blocks new ideas.

It is precisely the organizations that are praised as role models because of their learning capacity and adaptability that run the risk of establishing inflexible structures and processes. They get caught in a veritable "publicity trap." One example is the medium-sized manufacturer of scales in Germany that was highly praised for the self-organization of its assembly department, the elimination of warehousing, its dynamic development team, and its functioning continuous improvement process. The company's successes led to innovative structures being established for the long term. Anyone who visited the company when it was initially praised for its innovative processes would have noted with surprise five years later that nothing had changed. What contributed to the permanence of these structures was the fact that the company's own projects were repeatedly extolled in internal seminars and existing structures were thus continuously reinforced. The company became trapped in its own ideas and concepts.

The Learning Dilemma

Change processes confront organizations with a fundamental dilemma: on the one hand, the existence of a crisis can make it difficult to cope with the next crisis (Starbuck/Greve/Hedberg 1988). On the other, adaptation to a new situation can restrict the organization's ability to adapt to other situations in the future (Weick 1979). The successful design of a change process can make future change processes more complicated. The successful collective learning of a production process can prevent the process from being unlearned later on.[22]

In light of this situation, cynics might advise the companies that can afford to do so to deliberately engage in failed learning and change processes. Unsuccessful learning and failed change may be frustrating, but at least these companies will not establish rigid structures that are difficult to dissolve later on. As a result of failure, organizations remain open to the requirements of change.

However, because there are only a few organizations that are doing so well that they can afford to make failed learning and change processes part of their corporate strategies, most have no choice but to learn to live with this dilemma. This means that they must successfully learn and change, fully aware that the new structures and knowledge will at some point inhibit new learning and change.

---

22 See (Tsang/Shaker 2008) for an overview of the "unlearning" concept.

4.8. The Limitations of Planned Organizational Change

Identifying the blind spots of learning organizations can lead to provocative conclusions. Noncompliance with the principles of good organizational change cannot be attributed to employee opposition, the denseness of management, or the influence of the old hierarchical organization. There are very good reasons for employees to do the exact opposite of what is preached in most management literature and in the presentation slides shown by many consulting firms. The counter-principles to the principles of good organizational change are just as plausible as many of the principles of the learning organization.[23]

The Dilemmas of Organizational Change

Organizations that go through change processes are constantly faced with dilemmas. They require clear objectives, but they must be willing to stray from these objectives. It can make sense for employees to identify with processes, but this identification can impede the required change. For this reason, motivating employees through money alone can also be an effective strategy. Employee participation can unlock the potential for change, but too much participation can make it difficult to focus the organization. Self-organization can be helpful because solutions can be developed in the individual departments, but the organization of the change process by external firms can ensure a more original solution. Organizations need to create scope for innovation, but the formation of buffers often leads to organizational sloppiness. Although organizations are dependent on successful learning, it is precisely these successful learning processes that are responsible for failures. Learning avoidance can therefore also be a useful strategy.

The dilemmas discussed above highlight the fragility of all the organizational models that are geared toward organizational change. They

---

23 For this idea see the concept of the ambidextrous organization; see e.g. (March 1991); (Tushman/O'Reilly 1996); (Raisch/Birkinshaw 2008)

The Blind Spots of the Learning Organization

The principles of good organizational change	Counter-principles
1. Clear goals and visions • because they provide direction in change. • because they make coordination easier.	**1. Unclear goals and visions** • because they make for an open organization. • because they make it possible to quickly respond to environmental changes.
2. Employee identification with products and processes • because it strengthens the ties between employees and the organization in times of change. • because it gives employees a personal interest in both innovations and improved efficiency. • because it reduces the necessity for control.	**2. Motivation through money, company cars, incentives, etc., alone** • because it increases organizational elasticity. • because it makes it easier to order change from outside the organization. • because it allows for the broad deployment of staff.
3. Focusing on people • because it ensures that all resources are used. • because it allows employees to realize their full potential.	**3. People as a means to an end** • because the interchangeability of employees can make sense. • because members of organizations abstract from their own interests.
4. Communication, communication, communication • because linguistic communication mobilizes the views of many employees. • because it increases the quality of solutions. • because it reduces motivation and control problems.	**4. Hierarchy: preventing communication or permitting it selectively** • because it enables organizations to cope with complex tasks.
5. Self-organization • because it allows innovative solutions to be developed in the individual departments. • because it relieves top management of managerial tasks.	**5. Organization from outside** • because it paves the way for external solutions. • because it brings originality into play.
6. Maintaining resources for change • because it creates scope for change. • because it keeps errors from having a direct impact on the organization. • because it helps organizations cope with stressful situations.	**6. Eliminating buffers and reserves** • because it keeps organizations from wasting resources. • because it facilitates a streamlined organizational focus. • because it allows mistakes to be immediately recognized.
7. Learning • because it makes it easier to adapt to the environment. • because it allows successful structures to be formed.	**7. Learning avoidance** • because it makes for an open organization. • because it prevents set structures from being established that are difficult to eliminate.
→ *The principles of the learning organization*	→ *Counter-principles*

Table 5: The Central Dilemmas of Organizational Change

show that under conditions of great uncertainty, no methods of change can guarantee success. The learning organization is no exception. It is becoming increasingly difficult to distinguish between correct and incorrect action. No one is able to process information in such a comprehensive way—as an outside observer, as it were—that they are able to objectively say what a good or bad change process entails. The fundamental difficulty posed by change processes is that there are always good reasons to organize them in exactly the opposite way.

All That Learning Organizations Do Not Know

When managers, consultants, and scholars use the concept of the learning organization and thus rely on the principles of good organizational change, they accept a considerable degree of irrationality, ignorance, and amnesia. They forget that there are good reasons not to follow the rational principles discussed in the previous chapter, such as clear goals and visions, employee identification, the focus on people, communication, self-organization, and learning. They ignore the counter-principles to the principles of good organizational change and suppress the learning organization's many irrationalities.

What we are seeing here is the same construct of rationality underlying the supposedly optimal organizational structures of Taylorism, lean management, and business process reengineering. As discussed above, it was only possible to present these stability-oriented models as rational, efficient, and optimal by systematically ignoring and suppressing their drawbacks. The highly problematic side effects of the promoted best methods of organization were not detected due to the focus on rationality. As a result, the organization created a large number of blind spots for itself.

Similarly, the learning organization, as a model of good organizational change, can only be portrayed as a promising form of change because it ignores the side effects of rule-based change. It overlooks the fact that unwanted side effects always emerge when organizations follow the principles of good organizational change.

In the case of the learning organization, the knowledge-based company, and the agile enterprise, we see an interesting phenomenon. The proponents of these models are blind to their irrationalities, ignorance, and forgetfulness. They repeatedly praise the learning organization and the knowledge-based company as the most rational and adaptable forms of organization and systematically suppress their side effects. The names of the highly popular enhanced versions of these models—the "fast-learning organization" or the "fastest-learning organization"—are the magic formulas used to render these side effects invisible. To take up an idea by economist Albert O. Hirschman (Hirschman 1967), through these models, which are based on intelligence, knowledge, and learning, organizations merely perfect the ignorance of their own ignorance.

As Hirschman points out, these suppressions naturally have a function. It is precisely the change-oriented companies that would be overwhelmed if they constantly had to consider their own ignorance, irrationality, and forgetfulness. One can easily imagine the self-doubt that the members of a changing organization might feel if they were confronted with their own imperfections. These individuals need to convince themselves that they are in fact *not* ignorant, *not* irrational, and *not* forgetful. And what better way to do so than to persuade themselves that they are part of a learning, knowledgeable, and intelligent organization.

Outlook

This insight into the limited rationality of the learning organization can be frustrating for organizational managers, reformers, and consultants because it fundamentally undermines their self-image. They are expected to know how change works and which principles can be used to successfully carry out change projects. They are expected to establish a causal link between deficiencies, ideas, and actions—i.e., see the connection between causes and effects. Managers and consultants must be able to identify deficiencies and initiate processes that lead to the development of solutions. Consultants are in a position to demand money for their services because they claim to wield influence on the way deficiencies and solutions can be linked (Brunsson 1989, 224–25).

Given these limitations, we might demand that all rules of change management be consigned to the dustbin of antiquated management concepts. Theoretically speaking, the learning organization could be dismissed as a short-lived management fad. But perhaps there is a deeper meaning to the rules of change management, one that takes us beyond the question of what makes an organization particularly changeable. In the next chapter I will present a few thoughts on this topic.

5.
On the Benefits and Dangers of the Irrationality, Ignorance, and Forgetfulness of the Learning Organization

> "You have to do something new to see something new."
> *Georg Christoph Lichtenberg*

Given the problems with the rules of good organizational change in the learning organization model, it would seem obvious to take a closer look at the advantages of non-learning organizations or organizations that learn only to a limited degree. Organizational researcher Charles Perrow (Perrow 1979) has shown that many large organizations do not cope with turbulent, rapidly changing environments by adapting and learning, but rather by seeking to immobilize and control these environments. According to Perrow, due to their size and effective networks, such organizations are able to control their environment so effectively as to make short-term learning and adjustment processes unnecessary. Only when they are confronted with radical market changes do these organizations implement drastic "top-down" changes.

Psychoanalyst Fritz B. Simon (Simon 1997, 155) takes this logic one step further. According to Simon, it is not always useful for us to learn to adapt to our environment at short notice if we can assume that our environment will learn and adapt to us just as well. What would happen, Simon asks, if a woman refused to adapt to her husband? Is it not true that her refusal to learn would give her husband the opportunity to adapt to her? What would happen if students no longer learned to fulfill all the formal criteria of their programs and simply resisted the adaptation requirements imposed by their universities? Is it not true that their behavior would stir their universities out of their complacency and force them to change?

Ultimately, due to the refusal of people or even entire organizations to change processes or strategies at short notice in response to every signal from the environment, these people and organizations are able to make much more effective long-term changes. They do not repeatedly adapt at short notice to their environment, but engage in learning only after this environment has changed in fundamental ways. A wife engages in learning only when her husband has changed. Students learn only when university structures have been revamped.

The company that probably best embodies the "non-learning" organization as an organizational type is McDonald's. The restaurant chain's success is based on the fact that it offers identical products across the globe and takes hardly any notice at all of local particularities or its customers' special requirements. American customers of McDonald's can rightly assume that the hamburger they order in the center of Heidelberg is exactly the same size and has exactly the same ingredients and packaging as the one they ate in their hometown of Kansas just before leaving for Europe. Customers who try to make special requests such as "A few extra pickles on my Big Mac" or "I'll have a shot of rum in my Coke" will only be met with a shake of the head: these requests go against the restaurant chain's principle of paying no attention to individual requests.

McDonald's uses many of the principles than run counter to those of the learning organization. Thanks to clear hierarchies, only limited communication is permitted. The systematic elimination of buffers and organizational flab streamlines the company and prevents unnecessary deliberation at the franchise level. The frequently changing employees are seen as a means to the end of profit maximization and are motivated by money alone. At any rate, the McDonald's employee who is motivated by a particularly well-grilled burger, a super-clean McDonald's restaurant, or particularly friendly interaction with customers is probably more of an exception than a rule. The avoidance of decentralized learning keeps the entire organization open to radical change processes that are implemented from above.

The McDonald's principle has been copied by companies in many different sectors. Hotel chains such as Holiday Inn or Hotel Formule

I have set themselves apart from the competition by adopting the same efficiency standards as McDonald's. There are now "McStables" in which racehorses are trained and cared for according to standardized criteria, and in the United States, parents can place their children in "McChild" day care centers, where they are fed and looked in a supposedly efficient manner. Even the board members of telephone banking companies have proudly boasted that their banks are the "McDonald's of financial services."[24]

These McDonaldized companies do not adapt to their environments, but require their environments to adapt to them. McDonald's customers are expected to know that the choice of a meal is limited to the selection of a single or double hamburger, a small or a large bag of fries, and a meat or a vegetarian burger. This learning process appears to be one to which the environment (i.e., the customer) willingly submits. In line with the slogan "What's good for General Motors is good for the country," top executives at General Motors were long able to portray potential customers who did not buy the usual sedans as strange or unpatriotic. As one top manager put it, something "must be wrong" with people who prefer small cars and General Motors saw no reason to adjust to such market anomalies.[25]

The commercial success of this type of company is a result of the fact that much of the organization does not learn at short notice. The strength of this company type is that it largely ignores conflicting demands. As a result of its ignorance, the company is able to establish

---

24 See George Ritzer's insightful work (Ritzer 2011). The companies that are based on the McDonald's model do not represent revolutionary new organizations, even if this is often suggested. They have merely transferred to the service sector the Taylorist/Fordist organizational form that originated in industrial mass production. In other words, they systematically incorporate the assembly line principle that was invented by the Chicago slaughterhouses of the early twentieth century. The activities that directly create value are broken down into many small steps consisting of standardized, easy-to-learn hand movements, entries in computers, or sentences that can be mastered even by staff with little training.

25 See (Mintzberg 1989, 292). It can be confusing to call companies that work according to the McDonald's principle "learning organizations." One has the impression that all some companies feel they need to do to qualify as a learning organization is to open a Hamburger University in which students learn the best way to grill burgers. These companies apparently regard the awarding of university degrees in "Hamburgerology" as a sign that they are "intelligent" companies.

highly efficient, rationalized production processes into which workers can easily be integrated. Changes to the company's rules are complex and time-consuming and are implemented only by specialists at corporate headquarters. This results in great predictability for the company—as well as for the customer.

However, despite all the economic achievements of companies such as Holiday Inn, "McStables," and online banks, the model of the non-learning organization promises only limited success—as General Motors bitterly learned itself. So far there has been no wide-scale McDonaldization of the economy or society.

People who argue for organizations à la McDonald's that do not learn at short notice are only supporting the other side of the change dilemma. They are only emphasizing the counter-principles to those of the learning organizations (e.g., motivation through money alone, people as a means to an end, blocked communication, and learning avoidance) and creating their own blinds spots.

Due to the fact that the environment has become increasingly resistant to learning and increasingly unwilling to adapt to organizations, these blind spots can prove to be more lethal than the blind spots produced by the learning organization. Even quasi-monopolists like Microsoft have struggled with customers who no longer have the ability to learn and adapt that is necessary to skillfully deal with the random crashes of the Windows operating system or the kinks in the latest version of Word. Microsoft has experienced considerable customer defection, either in the form of customers using more exotic, less widespread programs or returning to the typewriter. Even institutions that support the population in its attempts to learn and adapt, such as public authorities in cities like Berlin, seem now to be struggling with their clientele's learning resistance and difficulties in adapting. City residents are increasingly unwilling to simply accept the authorities' decisions and are forcing these authorities to learn themselves.

For this reason it makes little sense to set the model of an organization that does not learn at short notice in opposition to that of the learning organization. Instead of a making simple appeal for the learning or the non-learning organization, for the principles of good or bad organizational change, we should take a closer look at the relationship between these two poles. Shifting the focus to the hidden functions of the learning organization concept can provide valuable new insights.

Refocusing on the Function of the Learning Organization Model

In the discussion of the learning organization we find a broad consensus on its objectives and purposes: to increase organizational efficiency, intelligence, and memory. The underlying assumption is that the broadest understanding of market conditions and decision-making alternatives provides the best foundation for organizational action. In short, the learning organization is described as the organizational form that can extract organizations out of the morass of irrationality, ignorance, and forgetfulness.

As is only logical, much of the literature deals with the question of how the learning organization can be made more efficient and intelligent and how the dark mists of irrationality and ignorance can be swept most effectively aside. Learning processes are studied and possible improvements are identified. New descriptive formulas for learning processes are offered, impediments to learning are analyzed, and ideas for overcoming them are developed. New organizational learning techniques are developed and innovative methods are tested in order to increase learning capacity.

The vast amount of literature on organizational learning certainly addresses the everyday concerns, hopes, and desires of organizational practitioners. There is agreement on the defined and promoted organizational goals—intelligence, reflexivity, and rationality—and attempts are made to find effective means to implement them: organizations should respond intelligently to complex environmental requirements. Rational processes of change must be established. The knowledge collected by the company or administration must be managed intelligently and the organizational memory of successes and failures must be preserved.

However, there is a real danger that the "learning organization" as an official objective is confused with real organizational processes. The consensus that "we want to be more efficient, intelligent, and capable of learning" threatens to distract organizations from the question of what actually underlies the debate on the learning organization. The agreed-on objective of learning suppresses everything that is at odds with this aura of efficiency, intelligence, and memory.

A central insight of the organizational research conducted in recent decades is that there is little sense in trying to understand organizations in terms of their official goals or purposes (Kühl 2013, 17). At first glance, this thesis may seem somewhat scandalous because in every company, administration, and association, goals are treated as self-evident fundamental assumptions. What employee would dare to cast doubt on official objectives and purposes?

In what follows, building on this insight from organizational research, I would like to fundamentally shift our perspective on the learning organization model. My intention is not to describe its official, oft-celebrated goals, but to focus on its hidden functions. My objective is to identify effects that are normally not intended or perceived by the concept's proponents (Merton 1957, 51ff.). My reasoning is that the official goals and purposes of the learning organization may be problematic, as shown above, but they nevertheless perform functions that give the concept a deeper meaning, even if these functions are at times difficult to see.

This approach has proved quite valuable when applied to social phenomena such as religion, magic, and crime. If we consider the official purpose of these social phenomena, we could easily do without all three in modern society. In the rational modern period, people have increasingly come to see religion as superstition. Magic is better left to the few indigenous groups that continue to practice it, and crime ultimately causes a great deal of unpleasantness not only for its victims but also for the apprehended criminals. However, in terms of hidden functions, religion, magic, and crime are quite meaningful: they increase the cohesion of society. People do not necessarily attend services in a mosque, synagogue, or church to strengthen the social ties of their communities, yet they perform this very function. The witch doctor's rain dance rarely produces rain, but it inevitably creates social cohesion in the village. Criminals do not usually steal old lady's purses to confirm social ideas about permissible and illicit behavior, but through the crime they contribute to strengthening these ideas and stabilizing society.

My thesis is that the model of the learning organization plays a similar role. Here, too, we see a rainmaker effect. If we consider only the official objective of this management method, we might as well toss it in the trash because of all the dilemmas that are associated with it. There are no clear, objective criteria for good or bad organizational change—they remain a pipe dream. However, just as religiosity, magic, and crime perform key functions in society, so, too, does the learning organization concept have an important, if not immediately recognizable, function for organizations: it motivates them try out new actions, even if is not entirely clear whether the organization will really benefits from them or not.

As I show in the first part of this chapter (5.1), this uncertainty is a result of the fact that the decisions relating to organizational change have become increasingly tricky and precarious. There are few clear criteria for determining whether or not change will lead to success. The direct and indirect consequences of an action are difficult to foresee. The central problem can be described as follows: if it is not clear whether a planned change process will be successful, organizations tend to delay making decisions and taking action. If it is unclear whether a decision is good or bad or whether the desired effects will be achieved, organizations tend to make decisions that have proven correct in similar situations in the past.

As I argue in the second part of the chapter (5.2), seen from this perspective, it can be important for organizations to develop mechanisms that convey the impression that new actions—i.e., transformation and change—are especially rational. Even if the probability of their success cannot be objectively calculated, it can be crucial for organizations to believe in the learning organization concept because of the increased uncertainty surrounding decisions. The focus on concepts such as the learning organization, the knowledge-based company, and the evolutionary firm are attempts to create this new form of rational organization.

The interesting point is that the necessary simultaneity of stability and change can be secured only through an intelligent form of self-deception. The model of the learning organization does not introduce rational forms of learning, change, or decision-making. Rather, under highly uncertain decision-making conditions, it promotes unknown new alternatives. What is also of interest is that the appeals for transformation and change are based on the suppression of the risks associated with change initiatives. It is precisely the "learning company"—which is presented as a more intelligent organizational form—that is marked by a high degree of irrationality, ignorance, and forgetfulness. This not only means that, as Nils Brunsson (Brunsson 1985) has convincingly shown, it can be useful to be irrational and ignorant, but also that the organizations that describe themselves as learning, intelligent, or knowledge-based produce a particularly sophisticated form of irrationality and ignorance.

An examination of the hidden functions of the learning organization allows us to see their problems in a new light. In the third part of this chapter (5.3), I will show that the learning organization risks falling victim to its own irrationalities, ignorance, and forgetfulness. There is a danger that the unwanted side effects of the principles of good organizational change that were described in the previous chapter will increase unnoticed. Despite the new need for action, the learning organization runs the risk of persisting in traditional behavioral patterns.

5.1. The Art of Treating Uncertain Knowledge as Certain

It is easy to demand that organizations not only do the "right things" but also "do things right," but how are managers to know what the right things are or how to do them correctly? And how can employees be certain that a decision is right at the current time?

Uncertainty—the Basis for Decisions

At first glance, it may seem to be a frustrating situation for decision-makers: even if they learn a lot, collect a great deal of information, and draw on many modern-day oracles, they can never be absolutely sure that a decision will turn out to be right or wrong. An assumption may prove incorrect, information may be faulty, or the oracle may be wrong once again.

Upon closer inspection, the decision-makers' frustration is unfounded. Uncertainty about right or wrong is characteristic of every decision. Ultimately, every decision and action is rooted in uncertainty. Without uncertainty, no decision or action would be necessary—or indeed even possible. Slogans such as "security instead of risk" may be suitable for the election campaigns of conservative parties, but as blanket instructions for organizations, they make little sense. Uncertainty is generally not a dysfunctional state that must be eliminated by certainty, but an existential precondition for all decision-making and action.

This is not really disadvantageous for decision-makers. If companies were always able to translate "objective" market conditions into action on the basis of generally accepted economic principles, they would not need to make any business decisions at all because correct action would result automatically from objective laws and market conditions. If the market sent clear signals at all times and there were clear ideas about correct organization, entrepreneurs would not be needed. Managers would be nothing more than the puppets of market laws and changing environmental conditions. Companies would probably closely resemble each other—after all, puppets move in similar ways.

If uncertainty did not characterize every buy and sell decision on the New York Stock Exchange, this temple of capitalism would be made superfluous. Based on the relevant learning and computational processes, all decision-makers would be able to bet on the "right" stock. Market fluctuations would no longer exist because everyone would already own the right securities. Investors who believe they can make safe decisions on the basis of sophisticated learning and computational processes often experience unpleasant surprises. This was certainly the case for the wealthy investors in the Long Term Capital Management hedge fund. The fund's managers, a select group of mathematicians and Nobel Prize-winning economists, were certain they had found a sure formula for increasing their money using derivatives. After suffering such devastating losses that they not only sank their own fund, but brought international financial markets to the brink of collapse, they were forced to realize that success in financial markets was not a matter of "calculating profits" but of "making decisions under uncertain conditions."

The situation is similar with product innovation. If it were clear which innovation were needed by a company in a given situation, innovation managers, product developers, and research departments would be superfluous. The innovation would only need to be implemented and launched. All the company would need to do is place the innovation on the designers' desks and wait for them to develop it to the point where it could be marketed.[26]

The logical conclusion is that if there is no alternative to a specific action, we do not need to make a decision or take action. If there were no uncertainty, organizations and decision-makers would be superfluous. An intelligent combination of machines and computers would be all organizations needed. They would only have to wait for the money to flow into their accounts.[27]

According to cybernetics researcher Heinz von Foerster, when we make decisions, we encounter a basic paradox. The only questions that need to be resolved are those that ultimately cannot be resolved. Everything else is a matter of complex (or less complex) calculation. Decisions therefore always represent personal attitudes in situations characterized by indeterminacy, indeterminableness, and logical undecidability. Managers make a subjective decision about market strategies because there are no strategies that can be derived directly from market

---

[26] All three examples are variations of the decision-making paradox discussed by Heinz von Foerster (Foerster 1992).

[27] This is a situation described in the work Meno by Plato. There is something absurd about searching for the solution to a problem. Either we know what we are looking for, in which case there is no problem, or we do not know what we are searching for, in which case we cannot expect to find anything (Polanyi 1966).

laws. They search through a cluttered warehouse of possible innovative products without really knowing what they are looking for.

This assumption certainly casts doubt on the usefulness of the established mechanisms of rational decision-making. However, from the perspective of job security, it can also provide some assurance to managers in a difficult situation: after all, the logical undecidability of decisions justifies the managers' very existence.

Exaggerating slightly, we might put it like this: if there was no organizational need to make decisions between equally attractive options, there would be no need for decision-makers. If there were no conflicting or ambiguous decision-making situations in organizations, these organizations would have no need for leaders because they would be able to continue their existing routines. If circumstances were completely identical, if no competing objectives existed, and if there were only one way to reach a desired goal, leadership—as Chester Barnard has argued (Barnard 1938, 21)—would be a matter of natural laws and would be entirely unnecessary. All the members of a management team could be assigned to work on production lines, behind the cash registers of fast food restaurants, or on cleaning crews in posh hotels, where they would need to perform only the routine tasks cropping up there. Presumably, the high salaries of managers include compensation for the fact that they must deal with this decision-making paradox in the interests of investors every morning.

The Hesitation to Try Something New

Because actions always point to uncertainties, a high degree of uncertainty always points to greater opportunities for organizational action. As the environment grows more uncertain, more actions are possible, they are more diverse, and there are more options for organizational decision-making. Furthermore, as uncertainty grows, employees have greater options for structuring their work and making decisions.

The central problem is that in times of great uncertainty, employees begin to hesitate. Ambiguities are exciting—so exciting, in fact, that there is a danger that no more action will be taken in the organization. Dilemmas, which ultimately represent uncertainties in the form of two meaningful, yet opposing, alternatives, can be a sure recipe for indecision and the inability to act in organizations. The desperate cry for "real decision-makers," "entrepreneurial thinkers in the company" and "real leaders" are a response to hesitation in the face of uncertainty. Organizations eagerly hope for managers who have the courage to make decisions even in uncertain times.

This problem of hesitation can be seen not only in manufacturing companies and service providers, but also in organizational consulting firms and research institutes. One example is the British consulting and research institute that received no follow-up contracts after completing one of its major projects. The market for introducing group work in administrations, which had long been lucrative, suddenly appeared to be saturated and the resulting uncertainty blocked the institute. It was entirely unclear which products and methods the institute could use to reach potential customers. Various proposals were dismissed with reference to the associated risks. Instead of trying out different strategies, the institute placed obstacles in its own path with discussions and reflection. Because of this block, at some point it seemed to make more sense to send out "rolls of toilet paper printed with any meaningful message" than to continue with further discussions.

In situations marked by increased uncertainty, organizations often stick to what has always worked well for them in the past. Particularly in times of great uncertainty, there appears to be a strong tendency to focus on established routines. Organizations remember the proven decisions of the past and apply them to the problems at hand. They retain the familiar way of working and restrict themselves to small incremental improvements. They do not know whether these routines will work, but at least they know that they have a fairly good mastery of the process.

Such response patterns are known from many companies. The market suddenly collapses, causing uncertainty in the company, which responds to the crisis not with innovations, but with hesitation. Instead of regarding the growing uncertainty as a chance to make unusual decisions, many companies focus on refining their proven routines. With the help of sophisticated cost reduction programs, they attempt to make the familiar approach more efficient and keep it.

The Logic of Resistance

The reluctance to change among employees, which is perceived as opposition, can also be attributed to hesitation in times of great uncertainty. Under uncertain conditions and in change processes, many employees point to the strengths of the existing system with comments such as "If it ain't broke, don't fix it," "We've always done things like that" or "That's just the way things are done here." The established routines and rituals are set in opposition to the risks of a change process that takes place under uncertain conditions. Proposals for change are torpedoed by references to negative experiences in the past or in other organizations: "We tried it once and it was a huge failure" or "Our office in Rome failed miserably with a similar program."

Many change initiatives are undermined by the claim that they are not viable at present. Proposals are described as "theory" which might seem persuasive in the abstract, but which is not feasible, affordable, or implementable in the real world. Initiatives are put off with comments such as "We'll get back to that later," "Good idea, but unfortunately the time isn't ripe for it yet," or "That's a great recommendation, but it doesn't suit our organizational culture."

Members of the organization often delay proposals for change with references to the opinion of "experts," well aware that a proposal that is discussed long enough will eventually end up in the proverbial dustbin. They point out that there is no legal foundation for the project or that it has not been assessed in terms of its full impact. Change projects are shunted to the periphery of the organization, where they can cause the least harm. In this way, ambitiously launched change initiatives become the subject of trainee programs, course material, and legal disputes.

The annoyance that managers often feel over this form of "resistance" can be explained by the fact that there is a deeper logic behind the objections. We cannot actually know whether the new is better than the old. Due to the paradox of the undecidability of decisions there is no ultimate way of determining whether a change will be useful or not. Every instance of refused change, every instance of inaction, can ultimately draw on this logic.

Managers, who are increasingly paid to implement change processes, face a difficult situation. Because it is nearly impossible to assess the effectiveness and success of a measure, all proposals for change risk being boycotted by opponents who point to their unclear benefits. Because it cannot be known beforehand whether an innovation will be successful, any attempt to force it through can be an extremely touchy matter.

The Vicious Circle of Uncertain Decisions

Due to the uncertainty that is perceived as increasing, organizations find themselves in a confounding situation. On the one hand, as a result of this growing uncertainty, they have ever more options for decision-making and action (and ever more H–H–requirements). On the other, the growing uncertainty makes the correctness of their decisions increasingly questionable. While there is a growing need for new decisions and actions, the basis of these decisions and actions is increasingly uncertain.

The question of how organizations can succeed in acting under such uncertain conditions has become crucial for their survival. The focus is shifting to the ways organizations can motivate their members to try out new actions—even if there are no clear criteria for success. The goal is to find a solution to a problem that was addressed two hundred years ago by the physicist and writer Georg Christoph Lichtenberg and that has become more urgent in the present day: If we wish to make something better, we must do something new. But if we do something new, we can never be sure that it will be better. How can we break this vicious circle and what role can the learning organization play in our efforts?

5.2. The Learning Organization Concept—Organized Self-Pacification

The key challenge for organizations is to muster the courage—even when extremely unsure about whether an initiative will succeed or fail—to embark on the adventure of change. To do so, they must break the vicious circle of greater options and a greater need for action, on the one hand, and the growing uncertainty about the correctness of decisions, on the other.

There is an effective way to overcome this circle: organizations must largely ignore the uncertainty that precedes every decision. They must take action and then persuade themselves that what they have done is correct and single-mindedly pursue the measure. The art of organization increasingly lies in treating uncertain knowledge as certain and taking committed and convincing action. It is becoming ever more important for managers to improve their ability to treat matters that should actually be doubted as certain. What is at stake here is the introduction of rationality and coherence where previously only uncertainty reigned.

Social psychologist Leon Festinger (Festinger 1957) was one of the first scholars to point out how necessary such ideas of rationality are for the well-being of human beings and organizations. According to Festinger, human beings are confronted with massive uncertainty in decision-making processes: Should I really marry John Smith? Wouldn't the country-style wicker sofa be a better choice than the leather sofa by Rolf Benz? Should I hire Robert Jones? Wouldn't it be better if the organization didn't change at all? In such situations, the decision-maker longs for reassurance.

In the case of a wedding, a new sofa, and a job applicant, it is relatively easy to reduce the uncertainty. We ask and listen to our friends, who tell us what a good choice we have made with our partner. The Rolf Benz brochure congratulates us on choosing a high-quality sofa and lets us know that we really could not have gotten anything better for the price. We pay a psychologist to test and confirm the suitability of Mr. Jones.

When faced with questions such as "Organizational change—yes or no?" or "If yes, in what form?" it is not quite as easy to eliminate the uncertainty. Here the assurances of a good friend, the comforting comments in a promotional brochure, or the tests administered by a psychologist might not do the trick. What is needed is a comprehensive model that offers us, in this uncertain situation, the certainty that change is the best path forward. Organizations need flexible myths of rationality ("myth" here being a less positive-sounding word for "model") in order to protect the change process from too much uncertainty when it comes to the "whether" and "how." Ideas about organizational change that are difficult to call into question are developed in order to support the changes that are made under uncertain conditions in organizations.

Glorifying Change

My thesis is that such myths of rationality are produced by the models of the learning organization, the knowledge-based company, the evolutionary firm, and the agile organization, which are seen as the "new best way of organization." These models support change and have a calming effect on organizations in troubled times. The learning organization and knowledge-based company concepts, which are in fact very difficult to criticize (after all, who can be against learning and knowledge?), make it possible to motivate people to experiment with new actions when faced with increasing uncertainty.

To this end, it is necessary that change as an objective and the good principles of change are seen as absolutes. Employees are sent to conferences on organizational learning, expensive studies are commissioned to document the learning progress in the organization, and advisers are sent through the company, the administration, the hospital, and (a real paradox!) schools to serve as ambassadors of the learning organization concept. In glossy brochures, principles such as continuous improvement in the organization, continuous communication, project management, further training, and ongoing feedback are preached as key success factors to illustrate the importance of change.

The Learning Organization Mitigates Conflicts over the Objectives of Change

If change is made into an organizational objective, the conflicts over the "whether" of change are reduced. The scope for protests and resistance to change is restricted by the glorification of learning and change. Nonchange becomes far less important as an alternative.

The postulate of a learning, adaptable organization robs employees of the ability to oppose change per se: we cannot close our minds to the idea of learning by the organization or else we are not a learning organization. We cannot oppose change because, after all, change is "the only stable element in our organization."

We need only consider the indignation felt by management over comments such as "That's not going to work anyway" or "We've never done things like that before." In a period in which organizational change and learning are glorified, such objections can get a person fired. It is quickly forgotten that with this attitude employees perform an important function in stabilizing the system and preserving its identity.

For the promoters of organizational change, change is rational. It can also be useful to market the learning organization as the best organizational form because it allows the organization to defend itself against sanctions and penalties if the change initiatives fail. The organization can then point out that with the attempted measures, it was merely following the model of the learning organization. The failure may be regrettable, but it is ultimately only an unavoidable consequence of a universally shared concept.

The Learning Organization— Providing Focus and Direction in Change Processes

Another function of the learning organization concept is to mitigate conflicts over the "how" of change and to provide direction in an organization undergoing a change process. The belief in the rules of good organizational change provides employees with the feeling that they are on the right track. It helps bring focus to change.

These ideas about the rational rules of organizational changes ensure that change processes can be coordinated with relatively little effort. A widely accepted, "rational" consensus exists on how change should take place. This frees the organization from constantly having to reach agreement in the event of conflicts of interest over the "how" of change.

The appearance of rationality that is conveyed by the learning organization concept creates the impression that the decision to change is not purely arbitrary or based on personal interests. Rather, it is ultimately derivable from basic premises shared by all parties. The calming function of ideas about good organizational change results from this trust-building aspect.

The Secret Function of the Methods and Formulas of Change

According to this thesis, the large number of management techniques and formulas that are oriented toward change perform an additional function beyond the officially stated objectives and purposes. The official aim of these methods and formulas is to present options for optimal organizational design. However, the concealed function of these fashions, formulas, and recommendations is to introduce natural-seeming simplifications under conditions of great uncertainty and thus to create enthusiasm for new, hitherto untried actions.[28]

Benchmarking: A rival company is unlikely to disclose precise, objective information on production costs—it probably only has approximate values itself. Nevertheless, it may be useful for an organization to find out whether the competition produces more cheaply. Whether this information is in fact true or not is of secondary importance. What is key is the result—namely, that streamlining potential is unlocked in the company. The function of benchmarking is fulfilled when it serves as "bench marketing" for streamlining and cost-cutting strategies.

---

28 See the interesting reflections on the function of management methods in (Abrahamson 1991; Abrahamson 1996; Abrahamson/Fairchild 1999).

Principles of good organizational change	Short-term increase in adaptability thanks to …
Clear goals and visions for the change processes	… the alignment of employees with a defined change-related objective
Employee identification with products and processes	… the mobilization of employees for clearly defined products and processes
Focusing on people in the organization	… activation through others' perspectives
Communication, communication, communication	… the extensive involvement of employees and the elimination of communication barriers
Self-organization	… the assignment of options for action to decentralized units
The maintenance of surplus resources for change	… the maintenance of surplus resources
Learning	… the establishment of a short-term "successful" change process

Table 6: Creating Focus with the Principles of Good Organizational Change

Quality standards: Adherence to the ISO 9000 quality standards does not mean that a product has a precisely defined quality, only that the organization has a thick quality assurance procedural manual. Nevertheless, it can make sense for a company to spend tens of thousands or even hundreds of thousands of dollars for such certification. With the ISO 9000 stamp, it can convince employees and customers that quality plays an important role in its operations.

Overhead value analysis: Even McKinsey's infamous overhead value analysis, which is currently being practiced under a number of new names, involves a similar trick in autosuggestion. Managers are required to quickly draw up a list of employee tasks. On the basis of this list, proposals are formulated for cost-cutting measures. The results of these studies are relatively unimportant. The critical point is that objective-appearing figures are produced that initiate organizational processes. Often the organization does not do exactly what is proposed in the studies, but the reference to the (often unread) findings and to McKinsey itself is enough to set change in motion.

The function of all these methods—ISO 9000, benchmarking, and overhead value analysis—is to initiate action by creating the illusion of rationality despite the existing uncertainties. With this in mind, deliberately overestimating the costs of ISO 9000 manuals, benchmarking studies, and consultants' reports may indeed be an effective strategy for management. If large sums are paid to create individual studies, it can make the members of the organization more willing to accept the rationality of the measure: "If that study cost half a million dollars, it can't be entirely unfounded." "If a consultant charges three thousand dollars a day, the recommendations she makes in the report must contain a grain of truth." As poet and painter Wilhelm Busch once said, "Upon closer inspection, our respect goes up with the price."

In summary, we can say that the fundamental strength of the learning organization model lies not in the many minor methods it uses to initiate learning processes within the organization, but in the fact that it makes "learning" and "change" into absolutes as organizational goals. The concept's central elements are its tendency to glorify change and the change this facilitates, despite decision-making uncertainty.

The Useful Irrationality, Ignorance, and Forgetfulness of the Learning Organization

The previous argument leads to an interesting insight. The strength of the learning organization concept is not that it leads to particularly rational decision-making processes, but, paradoxically, that the concept produces irrationality, ignorance, and forgetfulness on a large scale, which enables decisions to be made under conditions of great uncertainty.

The learning organization model creates an ignorance that ensures that organizations do not have to deal with the alternatives and side effects of change. Another way of saying this is that the learning organization refines the highly advanced art of suppression. It suppresses not only the potential side effects of an organizational structure, but also the side effects of change itself. It disregards not only the drawbacks of concepts such as lean management and business process reengineering, but also the problem of change per se.

The myths of rationality and the supposedly good rules of organizational change create a "hiding hand" that provides guidance when people try out new actions (Hirschman 1967). The positively charged model of the learning organization creates a protective ignorance that is an all-but essential condition for new endeavors because it conceals possible difficulties and thus ensures the necessary belief in success.

The fact that learning organizations are ignorant and necessarily forget even central aspects of their work—as well as the treasure trove of organizational experience—should in no way be understood as a fundamental argument against the learning organization. To the contrary, the labels "irrationality," "ignorance," and "forgetfulness" are frequently applied too quickly in order to discriminate against and disqualify an idea without taking note of the advantages these characteristics bring.

In the early twentieth century, various social scientists and economists pointed out that irrationalities, ignorance, and forgetfulness were essential for social systems to work. Without a belief in illusions, individuals, organizations, and entire societies would lack a stabilizing consensus and collapse. From this perspective, irrationalities, ignorance, and forgetfulness are no longer seen as passive dysfunctional processes, but take on a positive significance as the foundation of existing structures and relationships.

For example, historian John Sawyer (Sawyer 1952) determined that the only reason many large railway projects were undertaken in the United States was that their planners had grossly miscalculated costs. If the risks of many of these (ultimately successful) projects had been taken seriously, most would probably have been scratched in the planning phase. The only reason they were carried out was because of the ignorance of the managing directors as regards the actual risks.

This phenomenon can also be observed in many development aid projects. Before a project can be approved, its chances of success must be evaluated. This analysis gives the funding bodies the security that their investment is worthwhile. However, because the political, economic, and social contexts of such projects are often unstable, hardly any of them would be approved if realistic risk assessments were made. The probability of not achieving the officially declared objectives would be too great. It can therefore be convenient for development organizations such as the World Bank, the UN World Food Programme, and the Deutsche Gesellschaft für Internationale Zusammenarbeit to keep project review committees in the dark about projects in African or Asian countries if they want to launch them at all. Many of the projects do not achieve their desired objectives, but, as Albert O. Hirschman (Hirschman 1967) has explained, their initiators can at least hope that they will have additional benefits, even if not those originally intended, as a result of the deployment of money and staff. When measured against the original plans, the projects often fail. They are redirected, redefined, and ideally then lead to an initially unintended success.

Many product developments in companies are the result of similarly useful forms of ignorance, irrationality, and forgetfulness. Management teams and executive boards often concern themselves with decisions about negligible amounts of money for longer periods of time, but then approve large sums with little discussion. At times it is hard to avoid the impression that the length of time spent on a discussion is inversely related to the amount of money eventually invested. However, this behavior, which may seem irrational at first glance, has the hidden benefit of allowing risky product development projects to be tackled in the first place. Excessive advance scrutiny would probably have prevented the development of many currently successful products.

As regards the learning organization, the implication is the following: by making the principles of change into absolutes, organizations are able to suppress the risks associated with transformation and change. We might even speculate that the learning organization is more likely to motivate new actions than the demands made by management to try out new things or experiment under conditions of uncertainty. Organizational researcher Peter M. Blau (Blau 1955, 81) was among the first scholars to point out that under uncertain conditions, new behavior is produced to a greater extent by hidden functions than by officially promoted goals. At any rate, it is easy to imagine the opposition that would arise to new measures if managers were to announce that they, too, had no idea what course to set but believed the only chance the organization had was to experiment and try out something new.

The "Just Do Anything" Logic

The model of the learning organization, the knowledge-based company, the evolutionary organization, and the agile enterprise cannot guarantee that transformation and change will lead to success. However, they show the appeal of a type of behavior that at first glance seems irrational: Act *only* if you cannot be sure of the correctness, consequences, and side effects of your action. When confronted with the question, "What should I do?" it can make sense to answer, "I don't know, just do anything." As Karl E. Weick (Weick 1979) has written with an eye toward *Alice in Wonderland*, not knowing where you are heading is fine, as long as you know that you are heading somewhere. Sooner or later you will find out just where this somewhere lies and the benefits it brings.

It is precisely the irrationality, ignorance, and forgetfulness of the learning organization that allows organizations to emerge that are capable of experimentation. Existing structures are declared to be the problem and a demand is made to try out something new. As a result of irrationality, ignorance, and forgetfulness, the "new" is protected from questions about its meaning and potential for success. Understandable everyday questions such as "Is it worth it?" "Does it suit our organizational structure?" and "What will the supervisory board say?" are banned.

Under this logic, the desired goals are often not achieved, yet entirely new, interesting possibilities arise in the process. Christopher

Columbus may never have reached his desired destination, the Indian Subcontinent, but we can assume he was satisfied with the discovery of America. Despite spending pots of money on research, American drug-maker Pfizer never developed an effective cardiac drug, but it was so successful in selling its potency-enhancing drug Viagra—a byproduct of its intense search—that the unsuccessful research certainly paid off in the end.

Exaggerating slightly, we could say that the function of the learning organization is similar to that of the caribou bone used by the Naskapi people of North America (Weick 1979, 262). To determine where they should hunt, the Naskapi hold the shoulder bone of a caribou over a fire. As the bones heat up, cracks and spots appear that are interpreted by the tribe's experts as showing where the tribe should hunt. According to the Naskapi, the cracks and spots are divine signals with which the gods influence their hunting decisions.

Clearly, from a modern, enlightened point of view, the tribe's assumption that they have now made a rational decision is questionable. Nevertheless, their actions make sense. Deciding where to hunt on the basis of the caribou bone motivates the tribe to set off. There are no long debates about their destination; they are sure that they have made the right decision. And the strong motivation provided by a seemingly rational decision is not the only justification of this method. If the results of previous hunts influenced the Naskapi's decisions, the wildlife stocks in some regions would be so greatly reduced that no hunting would be possible there in the foreseeable future. In addition, the arbitrariness of the decision ensures that game does not adapt to the behavioral patterns of the hunters and thus systematically avoid certain regions during hunting season. Even if hunting is unsuccessful, the process is still useful. Because no single person determines where the tribe should hunt, responsibility for failure can be shifted to the gods, upon whom it is difficult to impose negative sanctions. The tribe does not have to deal with the time-consuming and socially problematic question of guilt.

The situation is similar with the learning organization. Just like the caribou bone, the learning organization concept provides security that the organization is on the right track. The chance that, using this concept, a company will be successful over a longer period is in fact no greater than the chance that the cracks and spots on caribou bones will lead the Naskapi to the largest herds. But just as the selection process used by Naskapi motivates them to act quickly and decisively in a given situation, so, too, does the learning organization concept motivate members of an organization to abandon the status quo and embark on the adventure of change.

5.3. The Learning Trap— the Learning Organization and Crises

A look at the hidden functions of the learning organization model opens up a new perspective on the dangers of such self-commitments. Organizations, due to their ignorance, irrationality, and forgetfulness, run the risk of *not* examining their change processes and thus ignoring changing environmental demands.

The Danger of Blind Spots

Stable rules for organizational change make it easier to evolve in a highly complex environment. However, these stable rules initially reduce the options for organizational action. Clearly, under conditions of great uncertainty, the assumptions about rationality in the learning organization model enable organizations to try out new actions; however, at the same time, they lead to risky self-commitments by the organization.

A look at the blind spots created by the seven principles of good organizational change makes this point clear. The commitment to an objective restricts what is imaginable in organizations. The employees' identification with products, processes, or organizational units limits the scope for change. The suppression of the interests of all employees makes it possible to chart a single course in the organization. The elimination of reserves reduces wiggle room. Successful learning establishes rigid structures.

Closer scrutiny of the blind spots of the learning organization leads to provocative conclusions. The systematic implementation of the learning organization model can cause an organizational disaster because, while these principles produce short-term adaptability, they create entrenched structures over the long term. The very structures that facilitate certain innovations prevent others. The rules that are designed to ensure creativity within the organization also place restrictions on this creativity. The structures that are intended to produce modifications are also the ones that prevent organizational change.

Over the long term, using the principles of the learning organization can be a highly risky proposition. Management cannot set clear objectives without running the risk of overlooking other opportunities. If management encourages employees to identify with processes, it faces the danger that the processes with which employees identify will become especially difficult to change. If the leaders of the organization rely on the broad participation of employees, they make it necessary for the organization to integrate various interests. By forming reserves, the organization risks increasing inefficiencies. The successful learning processes initiated by management bring the danger that the resulting structures will become so ossified that they are resistant to new learning processes.

To return to the story of the caribou bones of the Naskapi people: this decision-making system was long seen as a rational way of organizing the hunt, but the problem was that, as a method of "change management," it cut the tribe off from worsening environmental influences. When their hunting was unsuccessful over a period of several years, the system provided the usual explanations for this failure, such as, "The gods are against us." The tribe failed to see that the animals they had been hunting had been killed off and they should have switched to other sources of food long ago.

The principles of good organizational change	Unwanted side effects
Clear goals and visions for change processes	The organization lacks the flexibility to reach its goals when environmental conditions change
Employee identification with products and processes	The organization becomes less adaptable because processes become entrenched
The organizational focus on people	The organization is overwhelmed with the demands of its different members
Communication, communication, communication	Communication overload
Self-organization	The organization focuses on structures that should in fact be overcome
Maintaining resources for change	Excess resources result in waste and even self-obstruction
Learning	Successful learning establishes rigid structures and blocks subsequent adaptation processes
→ The principles of the learning organization	→ The blind spots of the learning organization

Table 7: The Unwanted Side Effects of the Principles of Good Organizational Change

Consequences for the Practice of Organizational Change

What are the consequences of these insights for the management of companies, administrations, hospitals, universities, and associations? In most organizations, the current models of good organizational change, including the learning organization, the knowledge-based company, and the evolutionary firm, will become worn with time. Even the currently promoted methods of change management, such as benchmarking, balanced scorecard, and the self-evaluation model of the European Foundation for Quality Management, will eventually lose their luster.

But that does not mean that most organizations will abandon either the models of good organizational change or the methods of change management. It is merely a matter of time before new, even more fascinating, and even more colorful models will emerge and new, seemingly more effective change management methods will be developed. It can definitely make sense for managers to use these emerging concepts and methods to safeguard change processes in organizations.

We can assume that the function of these new concepts and methods will be less to optimize decision-making processes and increase learning ability, and more to secure highly uncertain and risky change processes in organizations. The main benefit will be to allow organizations to break out of the vicious circle of unsure decisions and encourage them to test new organizational forms even under conditions of great uncertainty.

What seems important to me, though, is that management should keep in mind that these supposedly rational models and methods create a number of blind spots. As a result of these blind spots, the problematic side effects of a model or a method of organizational change may not be perceived. The side effects may worsen unnoticed and be discovered by staff only when they appear as an acute crisis.

6.
Beyond the Learning Organization—Managing the Dilemma of Organizational Change

"With us planning entails replacing chance with error."
Anonymous

Enlightened scholars and journalists often complain that organizations are inundated with the prescriptive literature and simple formulas of external consultants. They are surprised that self-help books, advice columns, training classes, and motivational videos have overrun not only society, but also organizational management, which usually cloaks itself in an aura of rationality. They note with indignation that many consultants and scholars produce only "hot air" and audaciously sell "old wine in new bottles."

A large number of authors are denouncing this hot air and this old wine in new bottles. They are calling for an end to the "one best ways" that offer formulas for successful business practice. They are criticizing the fact that the models and formulas for optimal action are merely directives that are applied independent of context and thus have only limited explanatory power in organizations.

It is probably only a matter of time before the focus of this enlightened literature will shift from static, stability-oriented models to models geared toward change processes. Instead of criticizing the blueprints for successful production, the authors will criticize the blueprints for successful organizational change. Instead of denouncing the formulas for good production, they will denounce the formulas for good change.

Despite all the justified criticism, this emphatic rejection of the models and formulas of change misses the mark. These models and formulas can be developed only at the expense of organizational blind spots and they thus conceal the contradictions and complexity of organizations. However, as I have shown, their weaknesses can actually considered strengths if they are viewed from the angle of motivating action. By concealing a complex reality, they fulfill a central function in decision-making processes.

In the first part of this chapter (6.1), I aim to introduce a concept that brings a healthy degree of skepticism to ideas about the learning organization and the good rules of change management. At the same time, this concept recognizes the value of such myths of rationality for change processes. In my opinion, the crucial point is to attempt to manage the prevailing contradictions in every organization in a situation-specific fashion.

When it comes to managing such dilemmas, it can be effective to use myths of rationality in the form of models and formulas in order to suppress the variety of contradictions. But it can also be useful to address the blind spots that have been produced by the different models and ideas of good organizational change and thus to create a more open organization.

The trick to managing the dilemmas described above is to organize the alternation between such closure and opening processes. As I argue in the second part of this chapter (6.2), this means abandoning the idea of a change process that can be planned, controlled, and calculated in detail. On the other hand, it does not mean abandoning the hope that one can have an influence on the design of the organization.

6.1. The Argument for an Overarching Perspective—Managing Contradictions

The point here is not to dispense with the diverse models of change, but to favor a metaperspective that does not make us into blind believers in these models and methods of change management, but allows us to selectively draw on myths of rationality in design processes. Instead of being fooled by the idea that the learning organization or the knowledge-based company is an objectively better organizational form and change management methods must be understood as certified, scientifically tested formulas that have been refined in practice, organizations should use such concepts in targeted ways because of their calming, focusing, motivating, and concealing effects. The goal is not only to harness the ignorance, irrationality, and forgetfulness produced by these methods, but also to become aware of their hidden functions at certain moments.

Suppressing Dilemmas

Conflicts and contradictions in organizations are initially perceived as unpleasant. They can have a devastating effect, particularly on change processes. It is therefore understandable why employees may wish to reduce them. It is also understandable why managers find "either-or" situations more acceptable than the "both-and" associated with polarities. Contradictions and dilemmas reflect unclear situations, and this lack of clarity is initially unsettling.

The traditional method for managing contradictions, conflicting goals, and dilemmas is simply to suppress them. Catch-22s, ambiguities, and instabilities are perceived as threatening to the status quo. Mechanisms are sought that promise to eliminate the dangers of contradictions, ambiguities, and uncertainty. The most common method is to concentrate on one aspect and ignore the other.

Models for this approach can be found in academia. In traditional business administration and management theory, in particular, we find a tendency to resolve all contradictions and conflicting goals. Evidently, any theory that searches for the Holy Grail of organization has little tolerance for contradictions, inconsistencies, and conflicting goals. Such theories are antagonistic to dilemmas. They signal a value system that requires employees not to disturb the status quo or—if the status quo is to be disturbed—that requires them at least to offer a coherent new concept.

The production of new models with the related attempts to define the proper rules of management is nothing more than an attempt to develop an undisturbed order. In the end, the formulation of good rules of organizational change is merely an elegant way to reduce the contradictions of organizational change processes. It is based on the conviction that although management cannot fully succeed in relieving its employees of contradictions, inconsistencies, and conflicting goals in their daily operations, it can at least rid change processes of these contradictions. Models such as the learning organization are used to signal to employees that while the order of the organizational structure can often be disrupted, a clear order must prevail in the form of change.

According to the consultants Friso den Hertog, Guido Philips, and Jan Cobbenhagen (Hertog/Philips/Cobbenhagen 1996, 44–45), despite all the progressive rhetoric, this understanding of organization calls to mind the age of mass production and mass consumption. It is based on the idea that the organization should always select just one principle: it should rely on organization by others or self-organization. It should learn or not learn. It should be centralized or decentralized. It should be oriented to functions or to processes. It should motivate employees through money or ensure that they identify with the processes. It should follow theory X or theory Y. By this logic, all elements, routines, and developments should be part of a rigorous, coherent model.

The solutions that are sought in such either-or organizations often tend to based on a "more of the same" strategy. The responses to the problems associated with change processes that were listed at the start of the fourth chapter exemplify this type of strategy—more communication, smarter consultants, more decisive managers, better change management, etc. Particularly in change processes, there appears to be little room for conflicting forms of organizational logic.

The Advantages of an Either-Or Attitude

Either-or attitudes, focusing on a single principle, and the systematic suppression of the consequences—all are helpful in many situations. It can certainly make sense to design change processes on the basis of principles such as clear goals, employee identification, participation, communication, and continuous learning.

Disregarding the dilemmas that are created by organizational change protects the organization from excessive self-doubt as to the decisions it has made. It helps conceal, from internal and external audiences, the inevitable contradictions surrounding actions. In many situations, it may be advisable to disregard dilemmas because of the demand made on managers to act decisively, rather than to act in a manner that is plausible from an organizational-theoretical point of view.

It can be advisable to conceal the contradictions of a change process, particularly in organizations in which considerable uncertainty exists concerning the path forward and in which change processes prove difficult. Management can project certainty by creating the impression that it knows which principles are needed to make a change project successful. In most organizations that use the learning organization model, it is precisely this calming function in change processes that is an important point.

One example is the medium-sized supplier of automotive parts that used the myths of rationality associated with the learning organization to conceal a large number of contradictions. The various changes in the company had given employees the feeling that management no longer knew exactly what direction the company needed to take in terms of its future development. It seemed unclear whether the company wanted to concentrate on its core business, become a systems supplier, move some of production to Eastern Europe, purchase other companies, or merge with other suppliers. This perception surely had a basis in reality, since many actions by management depended on chance circumstances and it is in general nearly impossible to define clear strategies for medium-sized companies in the turbulent supplier business. In this situation, management tried to create a minimum degree of certainty through the learning organization model. While acknowledging that it did not know exactly what the simple brilliant solution to all its problems was, it was able to signal that it knew how to organize the search. As a result, the company was able to initially tolerate the various contradictions of the change processes.

Disregarding contradictions and organizational dilemmas may even bring advantages for the consulting companies that as a rule have extensive knowledge of organizations. Consultants are often hired to create clarity in contradictory situations. They write flattering reports for top management in order to strengthen the selection of a particular course. Referring to the "best practices" in other enterprises, they propose pilot processes, define milestones, and encourage the elimination of alternatives in decision-making processes by supporting one group in the company with their expertise. The process that is set in motion by consultants in order to produce myths of rationality clearly has the goal of reducing contradictory situations in companies.

Consultants require a high level of certainty themselves, which cannot secured solely by an understanding of organizations that is based on contradictions. Consultants who explain all the possible paradoxical twists of their proposed strategies may disappoint clients who are looking for clear solutions to problems. We may complain that the only "tool" many consultants have is a hammer and they therefore tend to treat all organizational problems as "nails," yet it is precisely these hammer-bearing consultants who have enjoyed economic success since the mid-1990s—as exemplified by all the firms specializing in business process reengineering.[29]

The protracted and often vacuous discussions in consulting firms concerning which model and method to use perform the function of promising certainty to the client and inducing the firms' consultants to use a common language. Through flexible, change-oriented myths of rationality, organizations eliminate the diverse contradictions in change processes. They can convince themselves and others that they know exactly what needs to be done.

The Danger of Ignoring Contradictions

However, the danger of myths of rationality is that they make it impossible for organizations to use the suppressed and neutralized alternative actions. An opposite response that could be used effectively in a critical

---

29 The image of the hammer and the nail comes from psychologist Abraham Maslow. For a time it gained a new relevance in the United States and Germany because of the last name of one well-known promoter of business process reengineering, Michael Hammer.

situation is no longer available. It is only with a great effort that organizations can mobilize actions that run counter to the rules of good organizational change, including unclear objectives, motivation through money alone, the perception of employees as a means to an end, organization from outside, and the abandonment of linguistic communication.

Through myths of rationality, organizations run the risk of creating blind spots for themselves and producing unwanted, initially invisible side effects. The learning organization model is a textbook case of how short-term flexibility can be increased, but long-term learning processes are made more difficult, by principles such as clear objectives, employee identification, and continuous learning. It would therefore seem necessary for organizations to mobilize contradictions in a targeted way.

Increasing Complexity by Mobilizing Dilemmas

Organizations become more open when they permit existing contradictions. These contradictions can be understood as a force that dissolves clarity in organizations and thereby creates new opportunities.

If dilemmas, and ultimately conflicts, are permitted, the effect is to create complexity. Suppressed elements become evident, new ideas are developed, alternatives are formulated, and additional variants come into play.

What do these strategies for fostering contradictions and dilemmas look like in practice?

Recent consulting research has examined a variety of approaches to organizational blind spots. Their goal is to bring what is hidden to the surface and render it visible for employees by questioning what is *not* available in organizations.[30]

---

[30] Within the framework of Metaplan's structural analysis, we have long experimented with the systematic use of dilemmas as a mode of thought (see, for an early example, Metaplan 1997). Dirk Baecker (Baecker 1997) has also pointed out that questions such as "What is not available?" "What decisions are not made?" "Who is not participating?" and "What is not important?" can shift the focus to the blind spots of organizations.

The Method Of "Not"

By examining what is not, organization designers can counteract the tendency within and on the part of organizations to ensure controllability by systematically eliminating specific aspects of paradoxical, contradictory requirements. By asking what is lacking, organizations can bring to light those aspects of a dilemma that it has previously suppressed.

In orientation and search phases, it can be helpful for organization designers to initiate a change process that focuses on "not." They can make visible what—due to the organization's streamlined structure and rationality—was once considered insignificant, meaningless, trivial, or irrelevant and was therefore hardly noticed.

Using the "not" method, organizations can identify the blind spots they have created for themselves with the idea of an optimal organizational structure, the principles of good organizational change, and even with their daily operations: What goals are *not* pursued? What visions are *not* considered? What do employees *not* identify with and what should they *not* identify with? With what aspects of their identities should employees *not* contribute to the organization? Who does *not* communicate with each other and who should *not* communicate with each other? Where do we *not* want self-organization? Where do we *not* want buffers and reserves? Where does learning *not* take place and where should it *not* take place?

These questions serve merely as a point of departure for identifying additional critical issues in organizations through follow-up questions: Who should *not* talk to each other? Why should both of these employees *not* talk to each other? What would happen if they refrained from talking to each other? Who would then talk more? Is that what we want?

The preservation and promotion of dilemmas often brings conflicts to light. Using the "not" method, organizations can stimulate and strengthen conflicts and opposing interests. Such conflicts can have a positive effect on organizations, particularly on those that are usually too hasty with solutions.

The principles of good organizational change	"Not" questions
Goals	• What goals are not pursued in the profit center? • What objectives are pursued by management, but not by employees? • What visions are not taken into account?
Identification	• What things do employees not identify with? • Why do employees not identify with this process? • What should we not identify with because we would like to keep this process as adaptable as possible?
Integration of all aspects of a person's identity	• In what areas should employees not contribute to the organization with all aspects of their identities because routines are clear there?
Communication	• What type of communication will not be tolerated? • Who does not communicate with each other?
Self-organization	• What form of self-organization does not take place? • Where do we not want self-organization to take place?
Slack	• What opportunities do we not use to improve efficiency because we want to maintain resources for the possible requirements of change? • What mistakes are not recognized because we have too many buffers? • Where do we not want to have buffers and reserves?
Learning	• Where does learning not take place in the organization and where does little learning occur? • What learning processes should not take place?

Table 8: Questioning the Blind Spots of the Principles of Good Organizational Change

Against the Overestimation of Dilemmas—on the Benefits of a Metaperspective

However, it would also be a mistake to promote the use of dilemmas as *the* method of choice and to overestimate the value of working with contradictions and dilemmas. Rather, organizations should mobilize situation-specific contradictions. A metaperspective that does more than glorify the learning organization and mobilize dilemmas can be advantageous for creating new perspectives on change. It provides organizations with two courses of action, and these organizations can choose one or the other depending on the specific situation.

This approach allows for a much more relaxed use of the various models and methods of change. Organizations do not need to commit themselves to one model because it promises rationality and truth. Rather, they can avail themselves of its latent functions in change processes. From the viewpoint of these latent functions, it is of secondary importance whether use is made of the myth of rationality associated with the learning organization, the evolutionary enterprise, or the knowledge-based company. In addition, organizations can refrain from engaging in the unproductive debate (which cannot be settled objectively anyway) on whether the method of choice is the balanced scorecard, self-evaluations according to the European Quality Award, or benchmarking.

It is also much easier to alternate between methods because the goal is no longer to determine the ultimate—or even temporary—Holy Grail. The different models can be combined or used in succession. In the lingo of systems theory, they are "functional equivalents." They perform the same function in the attempt to focus the organization on the change process, and they are largely interchangeable.

Furthermore, a metaperspective can help us more quickly identify the different concepts' undesirable side effects. These side effects are unavoidable because management models, methods, and formulas lead to self-commitments by organizations that necessarily produce blind spots. If the learning organization and other concepts are grasped not as the new best method of organization, but, in an unspectacular and undogmatic way, are regarded as tools to suppress the problematic aspects of change, it is much easier to shift perspectives and recognize these self-produced blind spots.

This shift in perspective and examination of self-created blind spots makes a lot of sense, especially for organizations that have strongly immunized themselves against the side effects of organizational change through models such as the learning organization and through the rules of good change management. It can prevent the learning organization from atrophying into a particularly rigid, dogmatic organizational form.

The art of managing dilemmas lies in organizing the alternation between these two processes, which cannot be dictated by management, but is often a contested process within the organization. There are no patent formulas for determining when this alternation is useful, who should initiate it, and how it can be structured. The history of the company, the market environment, personnel structure, and the interests of all involved carry sufficient weight to render simple rules ineffective such as "a new model every five years" or "examine blind spots with every product launch."

6.2. Beyond the Dream of a Change Process That Can Be Planned

This management of dilemmas shifts the perspective on organizational change processes in fundamental ways (Aram 1976). The hope that the learning organization, the intelligent organization, or the agile enterprise will prove most capable of adapting to changing environmental conditions and effectively source, acquire, and share knowledge is replaced by a more complex conception of organizational change. Instead of engaging in an unproductive debate on whether the learning organization, the fast-learning organization, or even the mega-fast-learning organization is the proper vision of the future, organizations can use the ignorance and irrationalities of such models without completely sealing themselves off from the side effects of these myths of rationality.

Furthermore, the management of dilemmas is itself a concept with which blinds spots can again be created. The attempt to initiate suppressions and opening processes in a manner that is suitable to a given situation produces an overarching perspective while accepting problematic side effects. After all that has been covered so far, it would indeed be surprising if this were not the case—if the result were an organizational perspective not characterized by suppressions and ignorance.[31]

However, the main advantage of this management of dilemmas is that it takes us beyond misleading, abridged ideas about predictable, manageable, and controllable change. It allows us to bid farewell to the systematic approaches that follow the pattern of "clear objectives—comprehensive analysis—participatory development of solutions—implementation—robust evaluation." The ideas about predictability and controllability that are conveyed by the models of good organizational change and the instruments of change management have lead to simplistic ideas about change processes in many organizations. These ideas are based more on the official rhetoric of supposedly streamlined reorganization projects than on real-life organizational processes with all their contradictions.

The potential for managing organizational change lies not in perfecting the existing ideas about predictability and controllability or in creating more diverse models, more sophisticated change management tools, and more persuasive rules of good organizational change.

---

31 These ideas about the rational rules of organizational change, as well as the concept of dilemma management, are proposals for the next stage of the rationality "cycle"—for the replacement of the current rationality model by a new, more elaborate conception of rationality, which in turn will eventually be replaced itself. Almost all of the critics of traditional ideas about rationality have attempted to rescue rationality themselves. Herbert A. Simon once stated that human beings could never keep track of all the alternatives and consequences of a decision and were therefore only partly rational, but he then went on to claim that this limited rationality could be expanded through organizational structures. Charles E. Lindblom (Lindblom 1959) showed that rationality never existed before a decision, but then developed a model in which rationalities subsequently appeared on the market for political opinions. The garbage can model of decision-making, conceived as a fundamental criticism of other models by Michael D. Cohen, James G. March, and Johan P. Olsen (Cohen/March/Olsen 1972), views such decision-making processes as random combinations of solutions and problems within organizations. But it was also extended—by James G. March (March 1976)—to include a rationality model: In the "Technology of Foolishness," March develops a decision-making model that factors in the foolishness of all participants.

This would lead only to a greater discrepancy between the myths of rationality produced in this way and the reality of change processes in organizations. It is far more important to develop methodologies that take into account the paradox that every decision in organizations is relatively arbitrary because objective criteria for the right decision never exist from the start.

An Afterword on Methodology

The material for my books on organizational studies comes from three sources: my own research projects on organizations, which focus on a variety of concrete questions; consulting projects that have produced, as by-products, interesting insights into organizations; and descriptions of specific organizations by other consultants, managers, and researchers.

Because it is uncommon, especially in management literature, to "anonymize" the organizations that are discussed, I refer to them using their real names. If the examples in the published literature are anonymized, I use the names made up by the authors, even if the correct names are known to me. A few of the examples cited in this book are based on the empirical evidence I have gathered as a researcher, consultant, and, in some cases, even as a member of an organization. In such cases, I have either omitted the names of the organizations altogether or used fictitious names.

Bibliography

Abrahamson, Eric. 1991. "Managerial Fads and Fashions: The Diffusion and Rejection of Innovations." *Academy of Management Review* 16: 586–612.

Abrahamson, Eric. 1996. "Management Fashion." *Academy of Management Review* 21: 254–285.

Abrahamson, Eric, and Gregory Fairchild. 1999. "Management Fashion: Lifecycles, Triggers, and Collective Learning Processes." *Administrative Science Quarterly* 44: 708–740.

Almeida, Maria V., and António L. Soares. 2014. "Knowledge Sharing in Project-Based Organizations: Overcoming the Informational Limbo." *International Journal of Information Management* 34: 770–779.

Alvesson, Mats and Paul Thompson. 2005. "Postbureaucracy?" In *The Oxford Handbook of Work and Organization*, published by Stephen Ackroyd, Rosemary Batt, Paul Thompson, and Pamela S. Tolbert, 485–507. Oxford: Oxford University Press.

Aram, John D. 1976. *Dilemmas of Administrative Behavior*. Englewood Cliffs, NJ: Prentice Hall.

Argyris, Chris, and Donald Schön. 1978. *Organizational Learning: A Theory of Action Perspective*. Reading: Addison-Wesley.

Argyris, Chris, and Donald Schön. 1996. *Organizational Learning II: Theory, Method and Practice*. Reading: Addison Wesley.

Baecker, Dirk. 1997. *Das Handwerk des Unternehmers. Überlegungen zur Unternehmerausbildung*. Witten: unpublished manuscripts.

Barnard, Chester I. 1938. *The Functions of the Executive*. Cambridge, MA: Harvard University Press.

Beck, Ulrich. 2000. *What is Globalization?*. Translated by Patrick Camiller. Cambridge/Malden, MA: Polity Press.

Bennett, Charles A. 1969. *The Dilemma of Religious Knowledge*. Port Washington: Kennild.

Blau, Peter M. 1955. *The Dynamics of Bureaucracy*. Chicago: University of Chicago Press.

Brunsson, Nils. 1985. *The Irrational Organization: Irrationality as a Basis for Organizational Action and Change*. Chichester: John Wiley and Sons.

Brunsson, Nils. 1989. *The Organization of Hypocrisy: Talk, Decisions and Actions in Organizations.*
Chichester: John Wiley and Sons.

Castoriadis, Cornelius. 1987. *The Imaginary Institution of Society.* Translated by Kathleen Blamey.
Cambridge, MA: Polity Press.

Clark, Rodney. 1981. *The Japanese Company*. New Haven, London: Yale University Press.

Clark, Timothy, and Graeme Salaman. 1996. "The Management Guru as Organizational Witchdoctor." *Organization Studies*, no. 17: 85–107.

Cohen, Michael, James G. March, and Johan P. Olsen. 1972. "A Garbage Can Model of Rational Choice." *Administrative Science Quarterly*, no. 17: 1–25.

Commons, John R. 1924. *Legal Foundations of Capitalism*. New York: Macmillan.

Coser, Lewis A. 1974. *Greedy Institutions: Patterns of Undivided Commitment*. New York: Free Press.

Crozier, Michel. 1961. "De la bureaucratie comme système d'organisation." *Archives européenes de Sociologie*, no. 2: 18–52.

Cyert, Richard M., and James G. March. 1963. *A Behavioral Theory of the Firm*. Englewood Cliffs, NJ: Prentice Hall.

Durkheim, Émile. 1915. *The Elementary Forms of Religious Life: A Study in Religious Sociology*. Translated by J. W. Swain. New York: Macmillan; London: Allen and Unwin.

Eccles, Robert G. and Nitin Nohria. 1992. *Beyond the Hype: Rediscovering the Essence of Management*. Cambridge: Harvard Business School Press.

Evans, Paul A. L., and Yves Doz. 1992. "Dualities: A Paradigm for Human Resource and Organizational Development in Complex Multinationals." In *Globalizing Management: Creating and Leading the Competitive*

Organization, published by Vladimir Pucik, Noel M. Tichy, and Carole K. Barnett, 85–106. New York: John Wiley & Sons.

Festinger, Leon. 1957. *A Theory of Cognitive Dissonance.* Stanford: Stanford University Press.

Fincham, Robin. 2000. "Management as Magic: Reengineering and the Search for Business Salvation." In *The Reengineering Revolution? Critical Studies of Corporate Change,* published by David Knights, and Hugh Willmott, 174–191. London/Thousand Oaks/New Delhi: Sage.

Foerster, Heinz von. 1992. "Entdecken oder Erfinden: Wie läßt sich Verstehen verstehen?" In *Einführung in den Konstruktivismus,* 3rd ed, published by H. Gumin, and H. Meier, 41–88. München: Piper.

Foerster, Heinz von. 2003. "On Self-Organizing Systems and Their Environments." In *Understanding: Essays on Cybernetics and Cognition,* 1–20. New York: Springer.

Fox, Alan. 1974. *Beyond Contract: Work, Power and Trust Relations.* London: Farber & Farber.

Friedman, Andrew. 1977. *Industry and Labour.* London: Macmillan.

Garvin, David A. 1993. "Building a Learning Organization." *Harvard Business Review* 71, no. 4 (July, August): 78–91.

Gloger, Axel, and Ulrich Groothuis. 1994. "Völlig umgedreht." *WirtschaftsWoche,* no. 32 (5.8.1994): 54–56.

Granovetter, Mark S. 1973. "The Strength of Weak Ties." *American Journal of Sociology,* no. 78: 1360–1380.

Gunge, Søren Peter. 2000. "Business Process Reengineering and »The New Organization«." In *The Reengineering Revolution? Critical Studies of Corporate Change,* published by David Knights, and Hugh Willmott, 114–133. London/Thousand Oaks/New Delhi: Sage.

Habermas, Jürgen. 1984. *The Theory of Communicative Action.* Boston: Beacon Press.

Hampden-Turner, Charles T. 1992. *Creating Corporate Culture: From Discord to Harmony.* Reading, MA: Addison-Wesley.

Hedberg, Bo L. T. 1981. "How Organizations Learn and Unlearn." In *Handbook of Organizational Design,* published by Paul C. Nystrom, and William H. Starbuck, 3–27. Oxford: Oxford University Press.

Hertog, Friso den, Guido Philips, and Jan Cobbenhagen. 1996. "Paradox Management: The Fourth Phase of Innovation Management." In *Paradoxes Management: Widersprüche im Management—Management der Widerspruche*, published by Alfred Gutschelhofer, and Josef Scheff, 43–76. Wien: Linde.

Hirschman, Albert O. 1967. *Development Projects Observed.* Washington: Brookings Institution.

Höhn, Reinhard. 1935. *Rechtsgemeinschaft und Volksgemeinschaft.* Hamburg: Hanseatische Verlagsanstalt.

Hussey, David. 1998. *Strategic Management: From Theory to Implementation*, 4th ed. Oxford/Boston/
Johannesburg: Butterworth Heinemann.

Jackson, Brad. 2002. "A Fantasy Theme Analysis of Three Guru-led Management Fashions." In *Critical Consulting: New Perspectives on the Management Advice Industry*, published by Timothy Clark, and Robin Fincham, 172–190. Oxford/Malden: Blackwell.

Jos, Philip H., Mark E. Tompkins, and Steven W. Hays. 1989. "In Praise of Difficult People: A Portrait of the Committed Whistleblower." *Public Administration Review*, no. 49: 552–561.

Kanter, Rosabeth M. 1989. *When Giants Learn to Dance.* London: Simon & Schuster.

Kets de Vries, Manfred F. R. 1995. *Life and Death in the Executive Fast Lane: Essays on Irrational Organizations and Their Leaders.* San Francisco: Jossey-Bass.

Kieser, Alfred. 1994. "Fremdorganisation, Selbstorganisation und evolutionäres Management." *Zeitschrift für betriebswirtschaftliche Forschung*, no. 46: 199–228.

Krell, Gertraude, and Günther Ortmann. 1984. "Personal, Personalwirtschaft, Beschäftigungskrise." In *Betriebswirtschaftslehre und ökonomische Krise: Kontroverse Beiträge zur betriebswirtschaftlichen Krisenbewältigung*, published by Wolfgang H. Staehle, and Horst Albach, 321–338. Wiesbaden: Gabler.

Kühl, Stefan. 2005. "Exit: How Venture Capital Changes the Laws of Economics." Working Paper 3/2005, http://www.uni-bielefeld.de/soz/forschung/orgsoz/Stefan_Kuehl/pdf/Paper3.2005.-

Exit-How-Venture-Capital-changes-the-Law-of-Economics.pdf (10.05.2018).
Kühl, Stefan. 2013. *Organizations: A Systems Approach*. Translated by Philip Schmitz. Farnham/Burlington, VT: Gower-Ashgate.
Kupsch, Walther. 1926. *Gegenwartsfragen und Werksgemeinschaftsidee*. Berlin: Verlag des Bundes der Großdeutschen.
Laloux, Frederic. 2014. *Reinventing Organizations: A Guide to Creating Organizations Inspired by the Next Stage of Human Consciousness*. Brussels: Nelson Parker.
Lewin, Kurt. 1951. *Field Theory in Social Science*. New York: Harper & Row.
Lindblom, Charles E. 1959. "The Science of ›Muddling Through‹." *Public Administration Review*, no. 19: 79–88.
Luhmann, Niklas. 1964. *Funktionen und Folgen formaler Organisation*. Berlin: Duncker & Humblot.
Luhmann, Niklas. 1968. "Die Programmierung von Entscheidungen und das Problem der Flexibilität." In *Bürokratische Organisation*, published by Renate Mayntz, 324–341. Köln/Berlin: Kiepenheuer & Witsch.
Luhmann, Niklas. 1973. *Zweckbegriff und Systemrationalität: Über die Funktion von Zwecken in sozialen Systemen*. Frankfurt a.M.: Suhrkamp.
Luhmann, Niklas. 2000. *Organisation und Entscheidung*. Opladen: WDV.
Luhmann, Niklas. 2003. "Organization." In *Autopoietic Organization Theory: Drawing on Niklas Luhmann's Social Systems Perspective*, edited by Tore Bakken, and Tor Hernes, 31–52. Copenhagen: Copenhagen Business School Press.
Malinowski, Bronislaw. 1948. *Magic, Science and Religion*. New York: Free Press; Bacon Press.
March, James G. 1976. "The Technology of Foolishness." In *Ambiguity and Choice in Organizations*, published by James G. March, and Johan P. Olsen, 69–81. Bergen: Universitetsforlaget.
March, James G. 1988. "Introduction: A Chronicle of Speculations about Organizational Decision-making." In *Decisions and Organizations*, 1–24. Oxford: Basil Blackwell.

March, James G. 1991. „Exploration and Exploitation in Organizational Learning". In *Organization Science* 2: 71–87.

March, James G. 1994. *A Primer on Decision Making: How Decisions Happen*. New York: Free Press.

March, James G., and Johan P. Olsen. 1989. *Rediscovering Institutions*. New York: Free Press.

McLagan, Patricia, and Christo Nel. 1995. *The Age of Participation: New Governance for the Workplace and the World*. San Francisco: Berrett–Koehler Publishers.

Merton, Robert K. 1957. *Social Theory and Social Structure*, 2nd ed. Glencoe, IL: Free Press.

Metaplan Consulting. 1997. *Wir nehmen den Wandel von Strukturen in die Hand*. Quickborn: Metaplan Consulting.

Meyer, John W., and Brian Rowan. 1977. "Institutionalized Organizations: Formal Structure as Myth and Ceremony." *American Journal of Sociology*, no. 83: 340–363.

Miller, Danny, and Peter H. Friesen. 1984. *Organizations—A Quantum View*. Englewood Cliffs, NJ: Prentice Hall.

Mintzberg, Henry. 1989. *Mintzberg on Management: Inside Our Strange World of Organizations*. New York: Free Press.

Nelson, Richard R., and Sidney G. Winter. 1982. *An Evolutionary Theory of Economic Change*. Cambridge: Harvard University Press.

Nonaka, Ikujiro, and Hirotaka Takeuchi. 1995. *The Knowledge-Creating Company: How Japanese Companies Create the Dynamics of Innovation*. New York/Oxford: Oxford University Press.

Nystrom, Paul C., and William H. Starbuck. 1984. "To Avoid Organizational Crisis, Unlearn." *Organizational Dynamics* 13: 53–65.

Otala, Matti. 1995. "The Learning Organization: Theory into Practice." *Industry and Higher Education* 9(3) (June): 157–64.

Ouchi, William G. 1981. *Theory Z: How American Business Can Meet the Japanese Challenge*. New York: Addison Wesley.

Örtenblad, Anders. 2001. "On Differences Between Organizational Learning and Learning Organization." *The Learning Organization* 8: 125–133.

Packard, Vance. 1962. *The Pyramid Climbers*. London, New York: Longmans; McGraw-Hill.
Parsons, Talcott. 1965. "Some Ingredients of a General Theory of Formal Organization." In *Structure and Process in Modern Societies*, published by Talcott Parsons, 59–96. New York: Free Press.
Pascale, Richard T. 1990. *Managing on the Edge: How the Smartest Companies Use Conflict to Stay Ahead*. New York: Simon & Schuster.
Perrow, Charles. 1979. *Complex Organizations: A Critical Essay*. Glenview: Scott; Foreman.
Peters, Thomas J. 1994. *The Tom Peters Seminar: Crazy Times Call For Crazy Organizations*. New York: Vintage.
Peters, Thomas J., and Robert H. Waterman. 1982. *In Search of Excellence: Lessons from America's Best Run Companies*. New York: HarperCollins.
Pfeffer, Jeffrey, and Robert I. Sutton. 2006. *Hard Facts, Dangerous Half-Truths and Total Nonsense: Profiting from Evidence-Based Management*. Boston: Harvard Business Press.
Polanyi, Michael. 1996. *The Tacit Dimension*. London/Chicago: University of Chicago Press.
Raisch, Sebastian, and Julian Birkinshaw. 2008. "Organizational Ambidexterity: Antecedents, Outcomes, and Moderators." *Journal of Management* 34: 375–409.
Ritzer, George. 2011. *The McDonaldization of Society*, rev. ed. London/Thousand Oaks, CA: Sage.
Robbins, Harvey, and Michael Finley. 1996. *Why Change Doesn't Work: Why Initiatives Go Wrong and How to Try Again and Succeed*. Princeton: Peterson's.
Rottenburg, Richard. 1996. "When Organization Travels: On Intercultural Translation." In *Translating Organizational Change*, published by Barbara Szarniwska, and Guje Sevón, 191–240. Berlin/New York: Walter de Gruyter.
Sawyer, John E. 1952. "Entrepreneurial Error and Economic Growth." *Explorations in Entrepreneurial History* 4: 199–204.
Scott, Richard W. 1995. *Institutions and Organizations* Thousand Oaks/London: Sage.

Scott, W. Richard. 2003. *Organizations: Rational, Natural, and Open Systems*. Englewood Cliffs, NJ: Prentice Hall.

Senge, Peter M. 1990. *The Fifth Discipline: The Art and Practice of the Learning Organization*. New York: Doubleday.

Sharpe, Tom. 1976. *Wilt*. London: Secker & Warburg.

Simon, Fritz B. 1997. "Lernen—und wie man es erfolgreich verhindert." *GDI-Impuls*, no. 2: 3–12.

Simon, Herbert A. 1946. "The Proverbs of Administration." *Public Administration Review*, no. 6: 53–67.

Simon, Herbert A. 1957. *Models of Man: Social and Rational*. New York: John Wiley & Sons.

Simon, Herbert A. 1962. "The Architecture of Complexity." *Proceedings of the American Philosophical Society* 106 (6) (Dec 12) (Dec. 12, 1962 & Warburg, 1976)"um of the Bundeswehr in Dresden: 467–482.

Starbuck, William H. 1983. "Organizations as Action Generators." *American Sociological Review*, no. 48: 91–102.

Starbuck, William H., Arent Greve, and Bo L. T. Hedberg. 1988. "Responding to Crisis." In *The Strategy Process: Concepts, Contexts, and Cases*, published by James B. Quinn, Henry Mintzberg, and Robert M. James, 687–697. Englewood Cliffs, NJ: Prentice Hall.

Starkey, Ken. 1998. "What Can We Learn from the Learning Organization?." *Human Relations*, no. 51: 531–546.

Sturdy, Andrew, Christopher Wright, and Nick Wylie. 2014. "Managers as Consultants: The Hybridity and Tensions of Neo-Bureaucratic Management." *Organization:* 1–22.

Thompson, James D. 1967. *Organizations in Action*. New York: McGraw-Hill.

Toffler, Alvin. 1980. *The Third Wave*. New York: William Morrow.

Tsang, Eric W., and A. Zahra Shaker. 2008. "Organizational Unlearning." *Human Relations* 61: 1435–1462.

Tushman, Michael L./O'Reilly, Charles A. (1996): The Ambidextrous Organizations. Managing Evolutionary and Revolutionary Change. In: *California Management Review* 38, pp. 8–30.

Ward, John William. 1964. "The Ideal of Individualism and the Reality of Organizations." In *The Business Establishment*, published by Earl F. Cheit, 37–76. New York: Wiley.

Weick, Karl E. 1976. "Educational Organizations as Loosely Coupled Systems." *Administrative Science Quarterly*, no. 21: 1–19.

Weick, Karl E. 1977. "Re-Punctuating the Problem." In *New Perspectives on Organizational Effectiveness*, published by Paul S. Goodman, Johannes M. Pennings and associates, 193–225. San Francisco: Jossey-Bass.

Weick, Karl E. 1979. *The Social Psychology of Organizing*, 2d ed. Reading, MA: Addison-Wesley.

www.ingramcontent.com/pod-product-compliance
Lightning Source LLC
Chambersburg PA
CBHW020255030426
42336CB00010B/771